Galley
OUTDOOR COOKING

MAYFLOWER BOOKS, INC., U.S.A.
575 Lexington Avenue
New York, New York 10022

CONTENTS

ABBREVIATIONS

t. — teaspoon
T. — tablespoon
c. — cup
pkg. — package
pt. — pint
qt. — quart
oz. — ounce
lb. — pound

HOW TO BUILD A FIRE

A successful barbecue starts with a carefully built and controlled fire. Start the fire about 30 to 45 minutes before you want to begin barbecuing. This will allow the charcoal to burn evenly and to develop an intense heat. A charcoal fire may be started with several different methods.

Charcoal briquets are the most efficient. They give a longer, steadier and hotter heat. Briquets should be dry. For best results choose a standard high grade of charcoal or briquets. To start the fire, place twisted newspaper and enough kindling to burn for several minutes on the bottom of the firebox. Cover kindling with charcoal and pile in a pyramid. Ignite

paper in several places. Allow time for the fire to burn down to glowing embers.

Another method is to arrange charcoal in a pyramid and then to pour charcoal lighter fluid or commercial rubbing alcohol over it. Soak the charcoal thoroughly, then light with a long match.

A third method is to form a cup from aluminum foil. Fill with 2 or 3 spoonsful of solidified alcohol (sterno) and place on the bottom of the firebox. Add charcoal. Ignite alcohol. Let the charcoal burn to glowing embers. Then spread evenly over bottom of firebox.

3

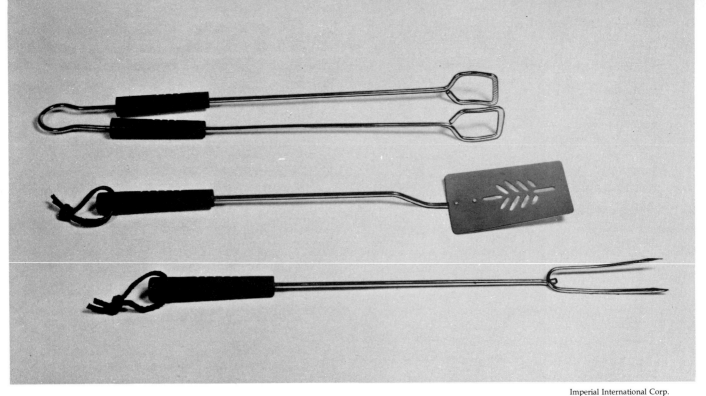

Imperial International Corp.

BARBECUE EQUIPMENT AND ACCESSORIES

The right equipment and tools add to the pleasure of barbecuing. Here are a few helpers to make your outdoor sessions more fun.

Aluminum Foil

Heavy-duty foil reflects back heat and speeds up cooking. It's also good for lining the firebox and for making drip pans.

Asbestos Gloves

Heavily padded heat-proof gloves for handling hot plates, skewers, charcoal, hot spits.

Basting Brush

A nylon brush with a long handle used for basting foods.

Briquets

Charcoal bricks used for food.

Braziers

A round or square flat pan supported on three legs in which charcoal is burned.

Broiling Baskets

Hinged holders for broiling small fish and meat.

Cooking Wagons

Elaborate braziers with work surfaces, rotisseries, hoods, shelves, smoke chambers.

Fire Starter

A liquid used to help ignite the fire.

Folding Grills

Small fireboxes with grill supported by folding legs.

Grid Brush

A wire brush with sturdy brass bristles for grill cleaning and polishing.

Hamburger Press

An adjustable aluminum press for forming thick or thin patties.

Hibachis

Iron or ceramic portable stoves with a fire-grill halfway down and a cooking grill on top. A damper regulates the fire.

Meat Thermometer

Used to check doneness of large cuts of meat.

Skewers

Wooden or metal pins, sharpened at one end, to hold meat together.

Tongs

Long steel grips for handling meat and poultry to prevent loss of juices.

OUTDOOR GRILL TIMETABLE

The time required for outdoor grilling will vary depending on the amount of heat, the distance from the flame and construction of the cooking device.

BEEF STEAKS (1 INCH THICK)
Rare — 8 to 12 minutes
Medium — 12 to 15 minutes
Well done — 15 to 20 minutes

BEEF STEAKS (1½ INCHES THICK)
Rare — 10 to 15 minutes
Medium — 14 to 18 minutes
Well done — 18 to 25 minutes

LAMB CHOPS AND STEAKS (1 INCH THICK)
Medium rare — 6 to 14 minutes
Well done — 18 to 25 minutes

LAMB CHOPS AND STEAKS (1½ INCHES THICK)
Medium rare — 8 to 16 minutes
Well done — 20 to 30 minutes

CHICKEN
Split — 25 to 45 minutes

HAM STEAKS
1 inch thick — 30 to 35 minutes
1½ inches thick — 35 to 45 minutes

HAMBURGERS
Rare — 10 to 12 minutes
Medium — 14 to 15 minutes
Well done — 18 to 20 minutes

FISH STEAKS
1 inch thick — 6 to 9 minutes
1½ inches thick — 8 to 12 minutes

COOKERY TERMS

Barbecue: To cook food in the open, whether on a spit or rack over hot coals or in a rotisserie basket, basting often with a highly seasoned sauce.

Baste: To moisten foods during cooking with fat drippings, water, oil or a sauce.

Broil: To cook by direct heat in a broiler or over hot coals.

Brown: To make food a brown color by frying, sautéing, broiling or baking.

Fry: To cook in hot fat. Cooking in a small amount of fat is called sautéing and cooking in a deep layer of hot fat is known as deep-fat frying.

Garnish: To add decorative color with small pieces of colorful food such as pepper, parsley, pimiento.

Marinate: To soak food in a seasoned liquid to tenderize or to add flavor.

Sauté: To cook food quickly with fat, butter or margarine.

Score: To partially cut narrow gashes through outer surface of food.

Sear: To brown meat quickly by intense heat.

LEMONADE REFRESHER

1 c. water	1 c. lemon juice
1 c. sugar	4 c. water

Combine sugar and water in a saucepan. Heat, stirring constantly, until sugar dissolves. Bring to a full rolling boil. Cool. Add lemon juice and water. Fill glasses. Add ice cubes.

ESCALLOPED CHICKEN

This has become a favorite for covered dish buffets and picnics.

Cook 1 stewing chicken until tender. Remove from bones. Strain broth. Make chicken gravy. Add seasonings to taste. In a buttered casserole dish, alternate layers of chicken with layers of dried or toasted bread cubes. Cover with gravy. Bake for 45 minutes in a 350° oven.

Mrs. Russell Beeman

PICNIC BURGERS

2 lbs. hamburger	1 onion
1 c. water	½ c. catsup
2 t. chili powder	Salt to taste
2 t. dry mustard	

Grind onion, add water with chili powder and mustard. Boil until onion is tender. Brown meat well, add catsup and salt. Simmer until done. Serve on buns with sliced onions, tomatoes, dill pickles.

Mrs. Emil Gubler

HAMBURGER ROLLS

1½ c. scalded milk
3 T. sugar
3 yeast cakes
2½ lbs. sifted flour
½ c. shortening
1½ T. salt
1½ c. cold water
3 eggs, slightly beaten

Mix scalded milk, shortening, sugar and salt. Cool by adding cold water. Add yeast cakes, mix. Add eggs and flour and mix. Place on well-floured board and roll out to thickness and shape desired. Place on greased tray and let rise until doubled in size. Bake 20 minutes at 400°. Makes 50 medium-sized rolls.

Mrs. Emil Gubler

HAMPER PICNIC

A picnic needs some basic equipment to keep the food hot or cold. An insulated cooler chest, vacuum bottles, and picnic hampers will hold the food until it is ready to be served.

MOCHA MILK

2 pts. coffee ice cream
½ c. chocolate syrup
¼ c. instant coffee powder
2 qts. milk

In a blender or mixer beat ice cream, syrup, coffee powder and a small amount of milk until well blended. Add remaining milk.

Note: Keep in thermos containers for outdoor eating.

To top off any cool, tall drink, add a slice of lemon or orange, a sprig of mint or a wedge of pineapple.

OVEN-FRIED CHICKEN

1 2- to 3-lb. chicken, cut up
1 stick butter
1½ c. flour
1 c. bread crumbs
1 t. salt
1 t. paprika
1 t. poultry seasoning
1 t. black pepper
1 c. canned milk

Wash chicken, drain. Season to taste with salt and pepper. Mix remaining dry ingredients. Mix chicken in milk. Roll chicken in flour and bread crumb mixture. Place in a large pan. Melt butter and spoon over chicken. Bake for 1 hour in a preheated 325° oven.

Mildred King

7

100-YEAR-OLD PORK CAKE

1 lb. salt pork	1 t. baking soda
(all fat)	1 t. nutmeg
1 pt. boiling water	1 t. cinnamon
4 c. sugar	1 t. cloves
½ c. molasses	1 lb. raisins
1 egg, well beaten	6 c. flour

Put pork through grinder, add boiling water and let stand until lukewarm. Stir in sugar, spices, soda, egg and molasses. Sift flour before measuring. Add flour and raisins to pork mixture, stirring until well blended. Pour into well-greased baking pans and bake for 2 hours at 300° until done.

Note: This cake can be eaten as soon as baked and cooled or it will keep for weeks. It is especially good for outdoor meals and picnics.

Rosalie L. Kennedy

FIVE-CUP SALAD

1 c. marshmallows
1 c. sour cream
1 small jar maraschino cherries, halved
1 c. chunk pineapple
1 c. mandarin oranges

Drain all fruits. Mix marshmallows and sour cream together and let stand several hours. When marshmallows are soft, mix well. Add cherries, pineapple, oranges. Stir well. Place in a covered bowl and store in refrigerator. When ready to serve, spoon on lettuce cups. Serves 8 to 10.

Glad Leonard

GERMAN POTATO SALAD

10 medium potatoes	¾ c. water
1 lb. bacon, diced	¼ c. sugar
1 T. flour	1 t. salt
¼ c. vinegar	1 small onion, diced

Boil potatoes with jackets on. Fry bacon until crisp. Remove bacon from pan and add flour, vinegar, water, sugar, salt and onion to bacon grease. Boil slowly for 5 to 10 minutes.

Peel and slice potatoes, add bacon pieces and pour above mixture over all. Serve hot. Serves 6 to 8.

Elaine Nelson

QUICK CABBAGE SALAD

⅓ c. cream
1 T. sugar
1 T. vinegar
½ t. minced onion
1 medium-sized carrot
1 cucumber, cubed
½ head medium-sized cabbage, finely diced
1 t. salt
Dash of pepper
½ green pepper, diced

Put sugar, vinegar, salt, pepper and cream in a bowl in which salad is to be served. Stir. Add minced onion and pepper. Grate carrot into dressing. Add cucumber. Add cabbage and mix well. Chill and serve.

Myrtle Warren

MACARONI SALAD

4 c. cooked elbow macaroni (½ lb. raw)
2 c. diced tomatoes
1 c. sharp grated cheese
1 c. mayonnaise
¼ c. sliced stuffed olives
2 T. grated onion
½ clove garlic
½ t. cayenne pepper

Rinse macaroni several times in cold water after it is cooked. Add remaining ingredients. Salt to taste. If cheese is somewhat bland, add more cayenne pepper.

Note: This salad should be made at least a day before it is to be served.

Mrs. Glenn C. Lindsey

Add cubes of cheddar cheese to your favorite hot potato salad; heat to melting. Sprinkle with chopped parsley.

MIXED-UP COLE SLAW

4 c. shredded cabbage
1 c. diced unpeeled red apples
1 c. pineapple tidbits
1 c. miniature colored marshmallows
½ c. seedless raisins

Mix all ingredients together. Add a sweet-sour salad dressing. All the extra ingredients transform cole slaw into something special.

Maysie Newsom

ORANGE CREAM

¼ c. confectioners' sugar
1 t. grated orange rind
2 T. orange juice
1 c. dairy sour cream

In a small bowl gently blend sugar, orange rind and juice. Gently fold in sour cream. Cover and chill. Serve as a dip with strawberries or as a sauce for fresh fruit.

PICNIC IN THE PARK

Let's have a picnic in the park
When days are warm and fair;
Let's find a lovely shady tree
To rest and linger there;
And if we care to take a stroll
Among the shrubs and flowers,
Our joy is doubled as we share
These pleasant sunny hours.
When mealtime comes around, we eat
Good food prepared with care,
Spread out upon a grassy slope
For everyone to share.
I'd like the joys of summertime
To last the whole year through,
For summertime means outdoor fun
With sports and picnics too.

Carice Williams

STRAWBERRY SHORTCAKE

1 c. flour   1 T. sugar
3 heaping t. baking   ¼ c. cold lard
  powder   (or substitute)
1 t. salt   Milk to mix

Sift flour, baking powder, sugar and salt. Cut lard into sifted dry ingredients. Add milk gradually, mixing with a fork. When a moderately stiff dough is formed, turn out on a floured board. Flatten the dough with a floured hand or rolling pin until about ½-inch thick. Cut into rounds with a small biscuit cutter. Bake in a 400° oven until nicely browned. When done, open and cover the two halves with mashed, sweetened strawberries. Top with whipped cream if desired.

Ruth Bunker Christiansen

EASY COCOA CAKE

2 c. sugar   ½ c. cocoa
1 c. shortening   1 c. sour milk
2 eggs   (or buttermilk)
1 t. salt   1 c. boiling water
2½ c. flour   2 t. vanilla
2 t. soda

Cream sugar and shortening, add eggs and soda and beat well. Add remaining dry ingredients and sour milk to creamed mixture and beat again. Stir in boiling water and vanilla and beat on low speed of electric mixer for several minutes. Bake in 2 layers or 13 x 9 x 2-inch oblong pan at 350° for 40 to 45 minutes or until cake tests done.

Mary Alice Campbell

PEANUT BUTTER COOKIES

½ c. lard   1 egg
⅓ c. peanut butter   1½ c. flour
½ c. brown sugar   1 t. soda
½ c. white sugar   ½ t. salt
½ t. vanilla

Cream the lard, peanut butter and sugars together. Add the egg and beat well. Sift the remaining dry ingredients together and add to the first mixture. Add the vanilla and form into small balls. Place on a greased baking sheet and press each ball flat with the prongs of a fork. Bake at 350° for 12 minutes. Yield: 4 dozen 2-inch cookies.

Bernice Peers

FAVORITE CUPCAKES

2¼ c. all-purpose flour   2 eggs
1 stick butter   1 t. vanilla
1 c. sugar   ¾ c. milk

Cream the sugar and butter. Add the eggs, then the flour alternately with the milk. Add the vanilla last and mix well. Put in 18 bake cups. Bake in a 350° oven for about 15 or 20 minutes.

Tiny E. Hammond

CHICKEN BARBECUE

PREPARING FOR THE COOKOUT

The grill should be located out of the wind, and if the day is hot, out of the sun. Plan to start the fire about 35 minutes ahead of cooking. Line the grill or floor of outdoor fireplace with heavy-duty aluminum foil. If there are vents in the bottom of the grill, cut out the foil to conform. Three pounds of briquets should be enough for the average cookout and will burn for 1½ hours. To start fire, gather briquets together over an electric starter, or mound them up and pour over charcoal lighter fluid.

Using tongs, spread briquets out into an even bed. Fire is ready when coals show gray spots. Cook shrimp first, then broil chicken. Fire will slow up somewhat towards the last hour, but chicken is best broiled slowly. When cooking is finished, the ashes and foil may be disposed of.

SHRIMP SCAMPI

  2 lbs. uncooked large shrimp
    (15 to 20 to a pound)
  2 cloves garlic
  ¾ c. butter or margarine
  ½ t. each: tarragon, rosemary, thyme
  3 T. lemon juice
1½ t. salt
   Freshly ground pepper to taste

Remove shell, leaving tail in place and devein shrimp. Mince or crush the garlic and combine with the butter or margarine and the herbs in a small saucepan. Let stand over heat for a few minutes to blend flavors, then add lemon juice. Tear six 12-inch squares of heavy-duty aluminum foil and arrange 4 or 5 shrimp on each. Pour over the garlic-butter mixture and sprinkle each serving with salt and freshly ground pepper. Bring foil up over shrimp, gathering edges together and twist at top to form a poke. Place on grill over a medium-hot fire for 10 to 20 minutes. Wrap French bread in foil and heat on the grill for 5 minutes, turning once.

COUNTRY TERRACE BARBECUE SAUCE

  ¾ c. diced scallions or young onions
  ½ c. chopped celery
  ¼ c. butter, margarine or salad oil
  2 15-oz. cans tomato sauce with tomato
    bits (or 4 c. chopped fresh tomatoes)
  ¼ c. chopped parsley
  4 T. brown sugar
  4 T. vinegar
1½ t. salt
  2 T. Worcestershire sauce

Sauté the onion and celery in the butter or salad oil. Add the tomato sauce or fresh tomatoes and simmer until vegetables are tender. Add remaining ingredients. Keep warm while basting chicken.

GARDEN TOMATO AND AVOCADO SALAD

  Lettuce or escarole
4 tomatoes, peeled
2 avocados, peeled and sliced

Wash, drain and refrigerate lettuce until crisp. Cut tomatoes into wedges. Sprinkle avocados with lemon juice. Refrigerate for approximately 1 hour. Arrange greens, tomatoes and avocados in a bowl.

HERBED FRENCH DRESSING

  ¾ c. olive oil or salad oil
  4 T. lemon juice
  1 t. dried tarragon
    (or 1 T. minced fresh tarragon)
  2 T. minced fresh chives
  1 T. fresh dill, snipped
  2 t. salt
   Pepper to taste

Combine oil and lemon juice. Add tarragon, chives and dill. Then add salt and pepper. Refrigerate 30 minutes.

Beat dressing with a fork, pour over salad ingredients, separating them with a fork so all are coated with dressing. Do not toss.

BARBECUED CHICKEN

Purchase broiler fryers, allowing a half or quarter chicken for each person. Rinse, pat dry and sprinkle with salt and pepper to taste. Place skin side up on grate about 5 inches above moderate briquet fire. Broil slowly for 10 to 15 minutes, then turn and broil skin side down until brown. Turn several times more and begin to baste about 10 minutes before chicken is done, since the barbecue sauce burns easily. Allow about 45 minutes total time for chickens weighing 1½ pounds, 1 to 1¼ hours for 2- to 2¼-pound chickens. Chicken is done when the drumstick can be twisted easily. Spoon remaining barbecue sauce over chicken when serving.

CORN ROAST

Informality is the keynote of a corn roast. Fill a big wooden pail with a bounty of ice cubes. Use paper accessories, too, so that cleanup time will be less of a chore.

CHUCK STEAK WITH ONION SAUCE

4¾ lbs. chuck steak, 1½ inches thick
    Meat tenderizer
    Onion sauce

Sprinkle steak with tenderizer. Prepare grill. Brush steak with the following Onion Sauce and cook on both sides on hot grill until done, 10 to 30 minutes.

ONION SAUCE

 3 T. onion soup mix
 2 T. sugar
½ t. salt
    Dash of pepper
 1 T. prepared mustard
¾ c. water
½ c. catsup
¼ c. cider vinegar
 1 T. lemon juice

Combine all ingredients in a saucepan. Simmer, covered, about 10 minutes.

Mrs. A. W. Eliot

ICED COFFEE AND TEA

Make coffee ⅓ stronger than usual and tea twice as strong. Try a slice of lime or lemon.

CUCUMBER SURPRISE

1 large cucumber
1 t. onion juice
⅓ c. French dressing

Wash cucumber. Slice paper-thin. Soak 20 minutes in salted ice water. Drain. Mix onion juice and dressing. Pour over cucumber. Stir. Add pepper to taste.

Mrs. V. A. Guiderly

BARBECUE SALAD

 1 head iceberg lettuce, cored, rinsed and drained
 1 cucumber, sliced
 2 tomatoes, quartered
 1 bunch radishes, sliced
 1 clove garlic, crushed
1½ c. corn oil
¼ lb. blue cheese
 2 T. lemon juice
 2 t. anchovy paste
 3 T. tarragon vinegar
1½ T. Worcestershire sauce
 2 T. bottled steak sauce
 2 T. dry red wine
    Salt and pepper to taste

Add garlic to the corn oil. Blend cheese with remaining ingredients. Remove garlic and add oil to the dressing. Mix well. Cut lettuce into bite-sized pieces. Add cucumber, tomatoes, radishes. Toss lightly with half of the dressing. Refrigerate remaining dressing. Serves 6.

Susan Lynn

The best steaks for grilling and broiling
    porterhouse
    sirloin
    rib steaks
    minute steaks
    filet

TENDERED BEEF

 1 3-lb. round steak or chuck roast, 2 inches thick
    Meat tenderizer
 1 5-oz. bottle soy sauce
¼ c. brown sugar, packed
 1 T. lemon juice
¼ c. bourbon (or brandy)
 1 t. Worcestershire sauce
1½ c. water

Sprinkle meat with tenderizer. Combine remaining ingredients. Marinate meat. Refrigerate meat at least 6 hours, turning once. Spoon on marinade often during grilling.

Lanita Fleischmann

STEAK TIMETABLE

1 INCH

Very rare — 6 to 8 minutes
Rare — 8 to 12 minutes
Medium — 12 to 15 minutes
Well done — 15 to 20 minutes

1½ INCHES

Very rare — 8 to 12 minutes
Rare — 10 to 15 minutes
Medium — 14 to 18 minutes
Well done — 18 to 25 minutes

2 INCHES

Very rare — 14 to 20 minutes
Rare — 18 to 30 minutes
Medium — 25 to 30 minutes
Well done — 45 to 60 minutes

2½ INCHES

Very rare — 20 to 30 minutes
Rare — 30 to 35 minutes
Medium — 35 to 45 minutes
Well done — 60 to 75 minutes

BARBECUED TOP SIRLOIN STEAK

3 lbs. top sirloin steak, 1½ inches thick
2 c. Burgundy wine
1 t. onion powder
¼ t. garlic powder
¼ t. black pepper

Place steak in a shallow bowl or pan. Add wine, then sprinkle with seasonings. Cover tightly and marinate overnight in refrigerator, turning once. Broil slowly on a greased grill approximately 4 inches from medium-hot coals, basting occasionally with the wine marinade. Serves 4 generously.

Andrew J. Shafer

To vary the flavor of steak, toss garlic clove halves on coals while grilling the steak. Or top with buttered sautéed mushrooms or green onions.

CRUSTY FRENCH BREAD

Slice bread diagonally almost through loaf. Brush with butter or margarine. Place bread on a double thickness of heavy-duty aluminum foil. Secure with a double fold on top and ends. Place to one side of grill, 5 to 7 inches above heat until bread is hot, about 12 to 18 minutes. Turn often.

GRILLED HAM STEAKS

2 uncooked smoked ham steaks, 1 inch thick
1 c. cider
3 T. brown sugar
1 T. dry mustard
3 whole cloves, crushed

Trim excess fat from ham. Score edges at 1-inch intervals. Place in a large skillet. Cover with boiling water. Parboil 5 minutes. Drain. Combine remaining ingredients. Blend well. Pour over steaks, marinate 15 minutes. Drain.

Grease grill with fat trimmings. Broil over medium coals until brown on both sides, turning and basting with marinade often. Grill until done.

Mrs. Charles Barry

ROASTED CORN

IN FOIL

If desired, husk corn, brush with melted butter and sprinkle with salt and pepper. Wrap each ear of corn in heavy-duty aluminum foil. Roast on a hot grill 20 to 40 minutes. Turn about every 10 minutes.

BROILED

Turn husks back without tearing them off the cob. Remove the silk, dip corn in cold water and replace the husks. Place on the grill. Turn often until they are heated through. Serve with melted butter and salt and pepper.

BAKED POTATOES

Scrub and brush firm, medium-sized baking potatoes with cooking oil. Wrap each potato in a square of aluminum foil, overlapping ends. Bake on the grill 45 to 60 minutes or on top of the coals. Turn occasionally if baking on the grill.

When potatoes are done, open foil. Cut a slit in the top, push ends to puff. Sprinkle with salt and pepper. Serve with sour cream or butter if desired.

CHEESY TOMATOES

2 tomatoes, halved
1 slice bread, broken into crumbs
½ c. shredded sharp process American cheese
2 T. butter, melted
  Salt and pepper to taste

Season sliced tomatoes with salt and pepper to taste. Combine crumbs, cheese, butter. Sprinkle over tomatoes. Wrap tomatoes in aluminum foil. Heat over medium-hot coals until warm. Makes 4 servings.

CHOCOLATE CHIP NUT SQUARES

1 egg, well beaten
½ c. sugar
1 t. melted butter or margarine
2 t. hot water
½ c. broken walnuts (optional)
1 c. chocolate chips
½ c. flour
½ t. baking powder
¼ t. salt

To the well-beaten egg add sugar gradually. Beat thoroughly. Add remaining ingredients in order listed, adding dry ingredients last. Turn into 8 x 8 x 2-inch pan. Bake 25 minutes in 325° oven. Cut in squares and remove from pan when cool.

Jean A. Williams

LEMON FLUFF PIE

1 baked piecrust
3 egg yolks, beaten
1 c. sugar
  Grated rind and juice of 1 lemon
3 T. hot water
3 egg whites, beaten

Beat the egg yolks until thick and lemon-colored. Gradually add ½ cup of the sugar, the lemon and hot water. Cook in top of a double boiler to thin custard. Add remaining sugar gradually to the beaten egg whites and fold into the custard. Fill baked piecrust. Brown lightly in 400° oven.

An orange may be substituted for the lemon if desired.

Mrs. Gene Smith

FOIL-ROASTED ONIONS

Peel a number of medium-size onions. Place each on double-thick aluminum foil. Dot with butter and sprinkle with salt, pepper and paprika to taste. Bring edges of foil together. Wrap to provide space for steam expansion. Seal with double folds. Cook on hot grill until tender, about 20 to 30 minutes. Turn about every 12 minutes.

Mrs. Ted L. Wright

RHUBARB SURPRISE CAKE

3 c. frozen, cut-up rhubarb
1½ c. water
1 c. sugar
1 3-oz. pkg. strawberry gelatin
1 2-layer pkg. white cake mix
2 c. miniature marshmallows

Bring to a boil rhubarb, water, sugar. Remove from heat. Add gelatin, mix, then set aside. Grease bottom of 13 x 9-inch baking pan. Cover with marshmallows. Prepare cake mix, using whole eggs. Pour batter over marshmallows, then pour rhubarb mixture over batter. Bake at 350° 45 to 50 minutes until lightly browned. Serve warm or cold with whipped cream or whipped topping.

Nettie L. Bornemeier

BARBECUE CHECKLIST

Barbecue grill	Wire brush
Charcoal briquets	Carving knife and fork
Lighter	Carving board
Basting brush	Dishes and silverware
Gloves	Napkins
Tongs	Smoke chips
Apron	Thermometer
Work table	Spatula

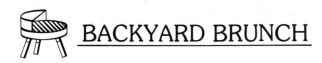

BACKYARD BRUNCH

Sunday brunch is an American tradition. It's a pleasant change from the hurried weekday breakfast and an excellent time to entertain. Relaxed and informal, brunch makes good food taste better and is fun for the hostess and guests.

OLD-FASHIONED PANCAKES

2 c. flour
¼ c. sugar
⅛ t. salt
2 c. milk or buttermilk
2 eggs
1 t. vanilla

Sift flour, sugar, salt together. Add milk, vanilla, eggs. Mix well. Batter will be very thin.

Fry in a skillet or on a griddle until light brown. When done, fill with applesauce, cottage cheese or apple jelly and roll up.

Rose L. Mills

COUNTRY PANCAKES

Capture fluffy clouds for flour,
Blend with golden oil of corn,
Fry with only blue sky sunshine,
Serve them on a summer morn.

Crown each stack with amber honey,
Sweet from clover fresh with dew,
Deck them all with country butter,
Now, good appetite to you.

D. A. Hoover

WHIPPED MAPLE BUTTER

½ c. butter
¾ c. pure maple syrup

With an electric mixer, beat butter until fluffy. Gradually add maple syrup and whip until well blended. Serve on pancakes or muffins. This can be stored in a covered container in the refrigerator until needed. Whip before serving to make it fluffy.

BACON AND EGG SUPREME

¼ c. finely chopped onions
½ c. butter
½ c. flour
4 c. milk
½ t. salt
⅛ t. pepper
1½ c. shredded Swiss cheese

Cook onion in butter until tender. Blend in flour, salt and pepper. Add milk gradually to form a smooth white sauce. Add cheese, stir until melted.

1 c. diced Canadian bacon
⅓ c. chopped pimiento
16 hard-cooked eggs, quartered
1½ c. soft bread crumbs
3 T. butter, melted
Toast points

Place half of the eggs in bottom of a 3-quart casserole. Add half of the bacon and pimiento. Pour half of sauce over this and repeat layers again. Cover. Bake at 375° for 45 minutes. Uncover and sprinkle with buttered bread crumbs. Bake another 15 minutes. Serve on toast points. Serves 16.

Mitzie Turck

To heat coffee cake on grill, wrap loosely in double thick aluminum foil. Place on a medium grill, 5 to 7 inches above heat, until cake is hot, about 12 to 15 minutes.

SOUR CREAM COFFEE CAKE

¼ c. sugar
1 t. cinnamon
4 T. chopped nuts

Mix above ingredients and set aside for topping.

¼ lb. sweet butter
1 c. sugar
2 eggs, beaten
1 c. sour cream
1 t. baking soda
1½ t. baking powder
1½ c. flour
1 t. vanilla

Cream butter and sugar. Add eggs, mix well. Add sour cream and mix. Sift dry ingredients. Add to mixture, beating in between. Add vanilla, mix well.

Pour half of the batter in an angel food cake pan. Add half of topping. Pour remaining batter and then add remaining topping. Swirl lightly with a spoon. Bake at 350° for 45 minutes.

Kathy Wiley

SCRAMBLED EGGS

6 eggs
¼ c. cream or milk
1 t. salt
¼ t. chili powder
3 T. sausage drippings, butter or
  margarine
1½ T. minced onion
  Dash of pepper

Combine first 5 ingredients in a mixing bowl. Beat lightly. Heat sausage drippings, butter or margarine in a large skillet over low heat. Add onions and heat. Add eggs and cook, stirring frequently, until eggs are done.

GRILLED TOMATOES

Slice fresh, washed tomatoes ½-inch thick, preparing as many slices as needed. Heat on first side in a lightly buttered skillet over moderate heat. Sprinkle with salt and pepper. Turn slices, season with salt and pepper and top with a sprinkling of shredded cheddar cheese and chopped chives. Heat until cheese softens. Serve.

GRILLED PORK SAUSAGE LINKS

Arrange desired number of pork sausage links in unheated skillet and cook slowly until links are fully cooked and lightly browned, turning sausages as needed to brown evenly, about 12 to 15 minutes. Save drippings. If cooking directions are given on package of pork sausage links, substitute for the above.

MELON FRUIT SALAD

1 cantaloupe
1 honeydew melon
⅓ of a watermelon
4 bananas
4 oranges
1½ lbs. strawberries
  Assorted fresh fruits

Dice all ingredients and mix well with juices from fruit. Add sugar to taste. Add about 2 small cans pineapple juice or lemon juice, or a can of ginger ale. Serves 6 to 8.

Bonnie K. Nalley

POOLSIDE PARTY

Celebrate any occasion with a cookout at your own backyard pool. You'll have a real treat when dinner includes an array of hamburgers.

OREGANO DIP

1 t. oregano	Few drops tabasco
½ t. grated onion	1 c. dairy sour cream
¼ t. salt	

Blend all ingredients into sour cream. Cover and chill.

VEGETABLE DIPPERS

Use the following relishes with a favorite dip:

  Radishes
  Celery hearts
  Cucumber petals
  Carrot crinkles
  Cauliflowerets
  Spring onions
  Broccoli buds
  Cherry tomatoes

WATERMELON BASKET

½ watermelon	1 qt. blueberries
1 cantaloupe	1 qt. cherries
1 qt. strawberries	3 limes

Make large watermelon balls from the half a watermelon, discarding seeds. Leave only the shell. Make smaller balls from the cantaloupe. With a sharp knife trim the edge of the watermelon shell. Cut 1-inch triangles all the way around, making a decorative sawtooth edge. Insert the knife slantwise, make an incision 1-inch deep. Next to it make another incision slanted in the opposite direction to finish the triangle point. Repeat all around, cutting one triangle out and leaving one standing up.

Fill the shell with the melon balls, adding strawberries, blueberries and cherries. Pile the fruit high in the shell. Decorate with 3 quartered limes and a few mint leaves. Chill before serving.

STUFFED HAMBURGERS

1½ lbs. ground beef
1½ t. salt
  1 c. seasoned, ready-mixed stuffing
  1 medium onion, grated
  ¼ c. butter or margarine
  2 T. lemon juice
  ¼ t. black pepper
    Dash of cayenne pepper

Mix hamburger and salt. Divide into 12 equal parts. Flatten each between pieces of waxed paper until about 5 inches in diameter. Leave each patty on paper. Combine remaining ingredients. Divide among 6 patties. Top each with a patty and press edges together with a fork. Broil on both sides until brown.

Edith Pikelny

Good toppers for burgers and frankfurters are catsup, mustard, barbecue sauces, pickle relish, horseradish, cheese slices, onion rings, chopped olives.

COOKOUT BURGERS

1½ lbs. ground beef
  1 c. instant nonfat dry milk
  1 t. salt
  1 egg
  1 T. instant minced onion

Mix together all ingredients. Shape into 6 large, flat patties and place in wire hamburger broiler. Cook slowly over coals, turning occasionally, until cooked to desired doneness. Serve on warm buttered sandwich buns.

VARIATION

Shape beef into 18 balls. Alternate 3 balls on a skewer with tomato and green pepper wedges, mushrooms, onions, and so forth. Place in broiler and cook as for burgers. Or wrap in heavy-duty aluminum foil and cook over hot coals.

Mrs. John G. Paley

BEEF BURGERS

    2 lbs. ground beef
      (round, chuck or hamburger)
  ½ c. finely chopped onion
    2 t. salt
  ¼ t. pepper
    2 eggs
      Melted butter or margarine

Combine all ingredients except butter or margarine. Mix well. Shape into 8 large patties. Brush with melted butter or margarine and broil slowly until brown on both sides, turning once. Cook to desired degree of doneness, 10 to 20 minutes. If cooked on outdoor gas grill, preheat on high flame 5 minutes, then reduce flame and broil meat as desired. If cooked over charcoal, broil meat on rack 4 to 4½ inches above a bed of low, glowing coals.

HAWAIIAN BURGERS

Combine 3 tablespoons each of prepared mustard and catsup. Stir in 1½ tablespoons soy sauce. Prepare Beef Burgers. Brush with sauce instead of butter or margarine. Top each with a heated, drained, canned pineapple slice.

GUACAMOLE-TOPPED BURGERS

    1 avocado   ¼ t. garlic salt
  ½ c. chopped tomato   4 to 6 drops
  ¼ c. chopped onion   tabasco sauce
    1 T. lemon juice   Dash of pepper
  ¼ t. salt

Mash pulp of avocado. Stir in remaining ingredients. Spoon mixture onto sizzling hot Beef Burgers. Heat.

GARDEN SALAD

1 c. cooked peas
1 c. cooked carrots, cubed
1 c. cooked celery, diced
1 c. cooked green beans, diced
1 t. onion, finely chopped
1 small cooked cauliflower, separated
1 c. French dressing
   Salt to taste

Marinate peas, carrots, celery, green beans and onion in French dressing. Chill 2 hours. Separate cauliflower flowerets and marinate separately in French dressing. Arrange lettuce on a platter or individual dishes, pile vegetables on lightly. Use separated cauliflower for a border around vegetables. Garnish with strips of red and green peppers. Serves 6.

Virginia Kraegenbrink

SALAD ACCENTS

   Sliced water chestnuts
   Croutons
   Asparagus tips
   Cherry tomatoes
   Crisp bacon
   Swiss cheese strips
   Ripe or stuffed sliced olives
   Green pepper rings
   Sliced hard-cooked eggs
   Pomegranate seeds
   Carrot curls

PIZZA PATTIES

1 lb. ground beef
¾ c. cracker crumbs
½ c. mozzarella cheese, grated
1 small onion, finely chopped
1 small garlic clove, minced
¼ t. oregano
   Salt and pepper to taste
1 egg
¼ c. tomato paste
¼ c. red wine

Combine all ingredients, mixing well. Shape into patties and barbecue over hot coals.

Jacqueline Shafer

BROWNIES

2 c. sugar   2 t. vanilla
⅓ c. cocoa   1½ c. sifted flour
1 c. melted butter   1 t. salt
4 eggs   ½ c. chopped nuts

Mix sugar and cocoa together. Stir in butter. Add eggs and vanilla and beat well. Sift flour and salt together and stir into cocoa mixture. Fold in nuts. Pour into a greased 15 x 10 x 1-inch jelly roll pan. Bake in 375° oven 25 minutes.

FROSTING

1 c. sugar
¼ c. butter
1 oz. sq. unsweetened chocolate
⅓ c. milk
   Dash of salt

Combine above ingredients. Bring to a boil, stirring constantly. Boil for 1 minute. Beat until of spreading consistency. Frost brownies.

Mrs. Walter Weichert

Sponge, angel and pound cakes make good summer desserts.

GEORGIA PEACH CAKE

1¼ c. sifted flour
¼ c. granulated sugar
½ t. salt
1 t. baking powder
½ c. solid shortening

Work the above ingredients together as for a piecrust. Mix and add to the above: 2 slightly beaten egg yolks and 2 tablespoons milk. Press into bottom of a 9 x 13-inch pan. Slice peaches and lay slices in rows on dough. Add the following streusel:

¾ c. sugar
2 T. flour
2 T. butter
⅛ t. nutmeg or cinnamon

Mix above ingredients together and sprinkle over peaches. Bake at 350° for 50 minutes.

Note: Apples may be used instead of peaches.

Mrs. G. R. Zachow

CRAB DIP

1 3-oz. pkg. cream   2 T. catsup
  cheese   2 T. minced onion
¼ c. mayonnaise   1 tin crabmeat

Combine all ingredients.

Karen Buchholz

CANTONESE PORK CHOPS

6 pork chops
1 8-oz. bottle sweet 'n sour sauce
1 14-oz. can pineapple chunks, drained
½ lb. snow peas
¼ c. sliced water chestnuts
1 medium-sized tomato, cut in wedges

Brown meat, add sauce. Cover. Simmer until meat is tender. Add pineapple, snow peas and water chestnuts. Cover and simmer until vegetables are crisp and tender. Add tomatoes, heat. Arrange meat, fruit and vegetables on serving platter. Thicken sauce if desired. Serves 6.

Margaret Gardner

ORIENTAL CHICKEN

1 broiler fryer, cut in serving pieces
2 eggs
1 T. water
1 c. cornstarch
  Salt and pepper

Sprinkle chicken with salt and pepper. Beat eggs and water until well mixed. Dip chicken into egg mixture, then into cornstarch. Dip into egg mixture again. Pour corn oil into large deep skillet to a depth of about ¼ inch. Heat over medium heat to 375°. Carefully put chicken into hot oil. Cook, turning once, 25 to 30 minutes or until light golden brown. Drain. Serves 4.

CHINESE RICE

1 c. long grain rice
½ t. salt (optional)
1½ to 2 c. cold water

Put rice in a heavy pan with a tight-fitting lid. Add salt and cold water. Set pan over high heat and boil rapidly, uncovered, until most of the water is absorbed. Stir often. Turn heat to low, cover and simmer 20 to 30 minutes.

CHINESE PATIO PARTY

Turn a backyard patio into an Oriental garden with Chinese lanterns, woven place mats, wind chimes and chopsticks.

BEAN SPROUT AND WATER CHESTNUT SALAD

2 c. bean sprouts, drained
¼ c. sliced water chestnuts
½ c. pineapple chunks
¼ c. slivered green pepper
1 c. mayonnaise
1 t. soy sauce
1 t. curry powder
  Toasted almonds

Combine bean sprouts, water chestnuts, pineapple and green pepper. Combine mayonnaise, soy sauce and curry powder. Mix through the bean sprout mixture. Arrange on lettuce. Sprinkle toasted almonds over top. Yield: 6 servings.

EGG DROP SOUP

2⅔ c. boiling, seasoned chicken broth
2 T. flour
½ t. salt
1 egg, slightly beaten

Heat broth to boiling point. Add flour and salt to egg and mix until smooth. Pour batter in a fine stream into boiling broth, stirring constantly. Serve immediately.

GLAZED CHINESE-STYLE SPARERIBS

4 to 5 pounds spareribs
1½ t. salt
½ t. garlic salt
½ c. apple or currant jelly
⅓ c. pineapple syrup
⅓ c. honey
1 T. soy sauce
½ t. ginger
¼ t. red food color
1 can (1 pound, 14 ounce) sliced
   pineapple, drained

Cut ribs into 3 or 4 rib sections. Place in shallow baking pan. Combine salts. Mix and sprinkle evenly over ribs. Cover ribs with aluminum foil, crimping foil firmly to edges of pan. Bake in 350° oven 1½ hours. While ribs are baking, combine jelly and syrup from canned pineapple, honey, soy sauce, ginger and food color in a saucepan. Bring to a boil slowly to melt jelly, stirring often. Simmer gently 5 minutes. Remove ribs from oven; remove foil and drain off drippings. Continue baking ribs, basting well with sauce several times during last 30 minutes of cooking. Serve with rice if desired. Yield: 6 servings.

CHINESE VEGETABLES

1 bunch celery or Chinese cabbage,
   sliced diagonally
½ c. green onions, sliced diagonally
2 T. salad oil
½ t. salt
¼ c. water
1 7-oz. pkg. frozen pea pods
3 T. soy sauce
1 T. cornstarch
1 T. water

Cook celery or cabbage, onions, oil, salt and ¼ cup water in a covered saucepan about 8 minutes. Add pea pods and soy sauce. Cook about 5 minutes. Drain, reserving liquid. Mix cornstarch and 1 tablespoon water. Add reserved liquid. Stir and cook until slightly thickened. Pour over vegetables.

FRESH COCONUT CAKE

1 c. sugar   ½ t. salt
¼ c. butter   2 c. cake flour
3 egg whites,   3 t. baking powder
   stiffly beaten   ½ c. freshly grated
⅔ c. milk   coconut

Cream butter, then gradually beat in sugar. Sift together dry ingredients. Add alternately with the milk to the sugar-butter mixture. Fold in egg whites and coconut. Stir well. Pour into a well-greased cake pan. Bake 45 minutes at 350°. Turn out on a cake rack to cool. Frost with a favorite frosting if desired. Or sprinkle with shredded coconut and chopped almonds.

ALMOND COOKIES

6 T. butter
1⅓ c. dark brown sugar
1 t. vanilla
1 egg, separated
2 c. sifted flour
⅛ t. salt
⅛ t. baking soda
⅛ t. cinnamon
¼ lb. blanched almonds, coarsely chopped

Cream butter. Gradually add sugar. Beat. Add vanilla and egg yolk. Beat until well blended. Mix and sift dry ingredients. Stir into butter mixture. Add nuts. Beat egg white until stiff. Fold into first mixture. Divide dough in half. Shape into two 1½-inch rolls. Wrap in waxed paper. Chill at least 3 hours. Slice thin. Bake on greased cookie sheet in a 375° oven 10 to 15 minutes. Makes 5 dozen.

FORTUNE COOKIES

¾ c. soft butter   3 eggs
2 c. sugar   1 c. sifted flour
1 t. vanilla   Paper fortunes

Cream butter with sugar until fluffy, then blend in vanilla. Add eggs, one at a time, beating well after each addition. Add flour. Blend. Drop 6 teaspoonsful of dough 2 inches apart on each greased and floured cookie sheet. Bake at 375° for 15 to 20 minutes. Remove from oven. Keep pan warm. Fold each cookie in half, slip fortune into fold. Keep top of cookie on the outside. Pinch points together. Makes 5 dozen cookies.

 # PORCH SMORGASBORD

Give a Swedish touch to the smorgasbord buffet with a blue and yellow color scheme and Swedish decorations. Light the table with candles.

CREAM OF MUSHROOM SOUP

1 can condensed cream of mushroom
  soup
1¼ c. milk
1 c. cooked mixed vegetables
  Salt and pepper to taste

Combine soup and milk. Stir until smooth and creamy. Add vegetables. Heat. Salt and pepper to taste. Serves 4.

SPICED COFFEE

½ c. brown sugar   ½ t. ground cloves
½ t. cinnamon   ½ t. nutmeg

Combine all ingredients. Mix well. Place 1 teaspoon in each cup. Add one strip of lemon and orange peel. Fill cup with strong, hot coffee. Top with whipped cream.

HOT CHICKEN SALAD

4 c. celery, cut up fine
4 c. chicken breasts, cooked and cut up fine
1 c. slivered almonds
4 t. grated onion
1 t. salt
1 t. monosodium glutamate
4 T. lemon juice
2 c. mayonnaise
2 c. crumbled potato chips

Mix above ingredients together gently and put into casserole. Bake at 350° for 40 minutes until hot and bubbly. Serve at once or freeze for later use.

Ann Dudley

SWEDISH BREAD

7⅛ c. sifted flour
2 c. sifted medium rye flour
¼ c. brown sugar
2 t. salt
2 t. caraway seed
2 t. grated orange peel
2 pkgs. active dry yeast
2 T. melted butter
2⅔ c. hot water

Combine flours. Mix 2½ cups of the flour mixture with all remaining ingredients except water. Gradually add hot water and beat about 2 minutes by hand. Add about 1 cup flour mixture and beat at high speed of electric mixer 2 more minutes. Add remaining flour gradually and knead until smooth. Place in a lightly greased bowl. Grease surface of dough lightly. Cover. Raise in a warm place until doubled in bulk, about 1 hour. Turn out on lightly floured board; punch down, divide into 2 equal parts and mold each into a round loaf. Put each loaf on a cookie sheet and make 3 slits across surface of each loaf with a sharp knife. Cover. Raise in a warm place until doubled in bulk, about 1 hour. Bake in a preheated 400° oven about 40 minutes.

MARINATED VEGETABLES

1¾ c. kidney beans, rinsed and well drained
1 10-oz. pkg. frozen mixed vegetables
½ c. chopped onion
½ c. chopped celery
½ c. sugar
1 T. all-purpose flour
2 t. dry mustard
¼ t. salt
½ c. vinegar
  Salad greens

Cook mixed vegetables according to package directions. Drain. Combine mixed vegetables, kidney beans, onion and celery. In a small saucepan, mix sugar, flour, mustard and salt. Gradually stir in vinegar. Stir and cook over medium heat until thick and clear. Cool slightly before mixing with bean mixture. Marinate several hours or overnight. Serve on salad greens.

Mrs. Jacob Baldinger

BROWN BEANS

1 lb. dry Swedish beans (or small navy beans)
1 c. dark corn syrup
¼ c. cider vinegar
1 T. salt

Soak beans in hot water overnight. Next day cook in same liquid 2 hours over medium-low heat. When beans are tender but not mushy, drain liquid and add remaining ingredients. Mix thoroughly. Cook uncovered over medium heat 30 minutes or until sauce has thickened.

Serve hot with Swedish meatballs.

Eleanore B. Malec

NUT MERINGUES

2½ c. toasted walnut halves	½ c. butter
	2 egg whites
2½ c. toasted pecan halves	¼ t. salt
	1 c. sugar

Preheat oven to 300°. Melt butter in a 15½ x 10½ x 1-inch pan in the oven. Combine egg whites and salt and beat until meringue stands in soft peaks. Gradually beat in sugar. Fold nuts into meringue. Spread mixture over butter in pan. Bake 30 minutes. Stir every 10 minutes. Cool. Store airtight. Makes approximately 2 pounds.

Mrs. Robert Hawn

SPRITZ COOKIES

¾ c. butter or margarine	1 egg yolk
	½ t. almond extract
½ c. sugar	2 c. sifted flour

Thoroughly cream butter and sugar together. Add egg yolk and beat until fluffy. Add flavoring, then flour. Mix until smooth. Put dough into a cookie press or pastry tube and force dough onto ungreased cookie sheets in shape of letter S or in rounds. Place about 1 inch apart. Bake in a 425° oven 8 to 10 minutes, until golden brown. Remove cookies from cookie sheets and place on cake rack to cool.

Carolyn Sanborn

SWEDISH MEATBALLS

2 lbs. ground beef	1 t. sage
½ lb. ground pork	½ t. nutmeg
1 c. oatmeal	¼ t. allspice
3 t. salt	1 c. buttermilk

Mix above ingredients well. Shape into balls. Brown on all sides, then bake at 350° for 45 minutes. Cloves of garlic may be speared on toothpicks and cooked with the meatballs, then removed before serving. Thicken meat juices and serve meatballs in their own gravy, or juices, as desired.

Laurie Williams

RASPBERRIES AND CREAM

1 qt. raspberries	4 T. cornstarch
1 to 1¼ c. sugar	4 T. water
2 c. water	

Combine sugar and water. Bring to the boiling point and simmer for a few minutes. Add fruit and boil gently 3 to 4 minutes. Mix cornstarch and water. Stir into raspberries. Bring to the boiling point, stirring constantly. Cook over low heat 3 to 4 minutes, stirring occasionally. Cover and cool. Serve with cream or milk.

SPICE CAKE

2 c. flour	1 t. baking soda
1 c. sugar	2 eggs, well beaten
4 T. butter	
1 scant c. buttermilk	1 t. cinnamon
	½ t. mace or nutmeg
2 T. molasses	

Combine sugar, spices, flour. Add butter, mix as for piecrust. Add molasses to milk. Add baking soda and mix well. Add to first mixture. Then add eggs. Pour into tube pan and bake at 375° for 45 minutes or until toothpick inserted in center comes out clean.

COOKING WITH SKEWERS

Shish kebabs provide a complete meal. The marinade tenderizes the meat and flavors the food.

SHISH KEBABS

    1 5- to 7-lb. leg of lamb
    1 clove garlic
    ½ c. chopped onions
    ½ t. oregano
    ¼ t. thyme
    ½ t. pepper
 1¼ t. salt
    ½ c. salad oil
    ⅓ c. lemon juice
    6 small whole onions, partially cooked
    6 tomatoes, quartered
    4 green peppers, quartered

Cut lamb in 1½-inch cubes. Trim off excess fat. Combine seasonings with salad oil and lemon juice. Mix thoroughly. Add lamb. Mix until each meat cube is well coated. Marinate overnight. Drain. Alternate meat with peppers, tomatoes and onions on skewers. Grill over hot coals until tender, about 20 minutes. Turn frequently.

Note: For rare meat, push close together when stringing on skewers. For well-done meat, leave a space in between.

RICE PILAF

1 c. rice	2 c. chicken bouillon
¼ c. minced onion	2 T. butter
¼ c. butter	Dash of oregano

Cook rice and onion in the ¼ cup butter until golden. Add bouillon. Cover and cook until rice is tender and liquid is absorbed. Add the 2 tablespoons of butter and the oregano.

SHRIMP KEBAB APPETIZERS

1 lb. green shrimp	¼ c. soy sauce
1 1-lb. can pineapple chunks	4 slices bacon

Cut bacon into 2-inch pieces. Place shrimp, pineapple in a bowl. Top with soy sauce. Set aside for 30 minutes.

Alternate shrimp, pineapple, bacon pieces on skewers. Place each skewer in the center of a lightly greased square of aluminum foil. Wrap. Bring up two sides of foil. Fold over top of skewer, using double fold. Double-fold ends. Place on grill. Broil, turning once, about 12 to 15 minutes.

SALAD BASICS

Head lettuce	Leaf lettuce
Bibb lettuce	Boston lettuce
Escarole	Watercress
Romaine	Celery lettuce
Curly endive	Spinach

SALAD ADDITIONS

Sliced water chestnuts
Tiny croutons browned in garlic butter
Chopped raw asparagus tips
Artichoke hearts
Crisp bacon
Sliced mushrooms
Ripe or stuffed sliced olives
Anchovies
Sliced hard-cooked eggs

BEEF TERIYAKI

    1 t. ginger
    1 clove garlic, minced
    ⅓ c. grated onion
    2 T. sugar
    ½ c. soy sauce
    ¼ c. water
    2 lbs. tender beef, cut into strips

Mix first 6 ingredients together. Pour over beef strips and put in refrigerator, covered, about 2 hours. Drain beef, arrange on skewers. Prepare grill. Cook on hot grill and brown meat slowly on both sides until done, about 10 to 20 minutes. Brush with marinade and turn often. Serve with rice.

Mrs. Alex Cary

MAKE-THEM-YOURSELF KEBABS

Make a choice from the following and place
on skewers. Cook, turning and basting occasionally, until done as desired.

Beef cubes
Lamb squares
Hamburger balls
Ham cubes
Sausage links
Frankfurter halves
Zucchini chunks
Bologna chunks
Canned or
    parboiled onions

Cherry tomatoes
Mushroom caps
Green and red
    pepper rings
Pineapple chunks
Small cooked potatoes
Stuffed olives
Banana slices
Spiced apples
Cooked carrot chunks

FRUIT DESSERTS

BROILED GRAPEFRUIT

Grapefruit
Light brown sugar
Maraschino cherry syrup
Medium-dry sherry wine

Cut fine meaty grapefruit in half. Remove pits and loosen the sections with a sharp knife. Sprinkle with sugar. Pour in some cherry syrup and wine. Broil until edges start to singe.

Edith Pikelny

PINK PEAR APPLESAUCE

6 cooking apples
3 ripe pears
1 2¾-oz. pkg. cinnamon red-hot candies

Core, peel and slice the apples and pears. Place in a heavy-bottomed saucepan with a tight-fitting cover. Simmer over low flame until fruit is tender, about 30 minutes, stirring occasionally to prevent sticking. Remove from heat and immediately stir in red-hots. Cool at room temperature. Chill. Makes approximately 1 quart.

Jacqueline Shafer

BAKED APPLES

Fill 1 8-inch square pan with apple halves. Pour 1 cup water and ⅓ cup brown sugar over apples. Sprinkle with cinnamon (or cinnamon candies) and nutmeg. Add 1 to 2 tablespoons tapioca. Bake at 350° for 45 minutes or until tender. Turn apples over, cool and serve.

Ardena Gassman

GRILLED BANANAS

Make a slit about 3 inches long in the skin of each unpeeled banana. Place a tablespoon of honey into each slit. Allow to stand ½ hour. Grill for about 8 minutes, turning often.

MINT-GLAZED PEARS

1 1-lb. can pear halves, drained
1 3-oz. pkg. lime or lemon-lime gelatin
1 c. boiling water
½ t. mint extract

Arrange pear halves in skillet. Dissolve gelatin in boiling water. Add mint extract. Pour over pears. Broil, basting often, until glaze begins to bubble and pears are lightly tinted, about 15 minutes. Serve warm or chilled.

Verna Sparks

MINTED GRAPEFRUIT

To one 16-oz. can grapefruit sections, add about 10 after-dinner mints. Chill thoroughly to blend the flavors. Serve when mints are dissolved.

June Kissinger

HONEY APPLES

1 c. honey
½ c. vinegar
1 T. butter
3 c. apples

Heat honey, vinegar, butter. When hot and bubbling, add peeled and thinly sliced apples. Watch carefully, simmering until apples are transparent and tender. Skim out of sauce when done.

Serve chilled or hot as a relish with pork or ham, or as a dessert with cream or ice cream.

Maysie Newsom

It's a good idea to serve frozen fruits with some ice crystals still in them; the texture will be firmer — more like that of fresh fruits.

DESSERT DELIGHTS

Sliced oranges sprinkled with coconut.

Thawed frozen raspberries served on ice cream or on sliced fresh pears.

Melon balls garnished with mint and served with lemon or lime wedges.

A fresh fruit cup with a sauce of diluted crème de menthe.

PINK FRUIT PUNCH

6 c. sugar
6 c. water
2 pkgs. strawberry Kool-Aid
1 12-oz. can frozen lemon juice
1 12-oz. can frozen orange juice
1 46-oz. can pineapple juice

Combine sugar and water. Boil for 5 minutes. Cool. Add remaining ingredients. When ready to serve the punch add 2 quarts of ginger ale plus enough water to make three gallons.

Mrs. Robert E. O'Leary

COCONUT MILK

To 2 cups boiling water, add 4 cups grated fresh coconut. Strain. Keep refrigerated.

PAN-FRIED FRUIT

BANANAS

Peel all-yellow bananas and cut in half lengthwise. Melt 3 tablespoons butter in a skillet. Fry bananas until tender, turning to brown evenly, about 8 to 10 minutes. Sprinkle with salt.

PINEAPPLE RINGS

Pare, slice and core fresh pineapple. Cook as for bananas, frying 10 to 12 minutes. Sprinkle with 2 tablespoons brown sugar.

Janis M. Phillips

LUAU RIBS

4 lbs. spareribs	¾ c. water
¾ c. cornstarch	¾ c. pineapple juice
¼ c. molasses	1 can pineapple
¼ c. soy sauce	chunks
½ c. sugar	2 green peppers,
¾ c. vinegar	cubed

Cut spareribs into 1½-inch strips. Brown in heavy skillet or Dutch oven. Combine cornstarch, molasses, soy sauce. Spread on ribs. Rebrown in hot fat. Combine sugar, vinegar, water and juice and heat until sugar dissolves. Pour over ribs. Cover. Cook 20 to 30 minutes. Add pineapple and green pepper and recover. Simmer a little longer.

HAWAIIAN PARTY

Have a backyard party, Hawaiian style. Greet guests with flower leis. For attire, suggest muu-muus and brightly colored shirts. Accent the table with flowers and fruit.

SHRIMP AND CRAB SPREAD

1 8-oz. can shrimp
1 8-oz. can crabmeat
2 8-oz. pkgs. cream cheese
1 medium onion, chopped

Combine above ingredients. Heat for 30 minutes in a 350° oven. Stir once. Serve hot with crackers.

Mrs. N. C. Kitchin

SHRIMP SALAD

1 small can cleaned shrimp
1 c. diced celery, including leaves
¾ c. sliced stuffed olives
 Creamy salad dressing

Cut shrimp into small pieces, add diced celery and sliced olives. Mix. Add enough creamy salad dressing to coat entire mixture. Place lettuce leaves on salad plates, add 2 tablespoons of shrimp mixture, sprinkle with paprika.

Mrs. W. J. Demerly

PEAS AND MUSHROOMS

1 10-oz. pkg. frozen peas
3 T. butter or margarine
1 3-oz. can broiled, sliced mushrooms,
 drained
 Salt and pepper to taste

Place frozen peas on a large square of aluminum foil. Season with a little salt and pepper and top with butter and drained mushrooms. Bring edges of foil up. Leave a little space for expansion of steam. Seal tightly with double fold. Place package over hot coals about 10 to 15 minutes. Turn occasionally. Serves 4.

CHICKEN AND RICE

2 lbs. chicken, cut up
1 c. uncooked rice
1 can cream of mushroom soup
2½ cans water
2 pkgs. dry onion soup mix

Mix all ingredients except chicken in a large baking dish. Place chicken on top of mixture. Cover with foil and bake at 325° for 2 hours. Uncover for last ½ hour of baking time.

Bonnie Ellsworth

HAWAIIAN HAM

1 boned, fully cooked whole or half ham
1 8½-oz. can crushed pineapple, undrained
½ c. orange marmalade
1 T. cornstarch
1 T. vinegar
2 t. prepared mustard
⅓ c. flaked coconut
   Assorted fresh fruits (optional)
   Mint (optional)

Remove wrapper and inside casing from ham. Place ham on a rack in a shallow, uncovered baking pan. Heat in a 325°oven as directed on ham label or until meat thermometer inserted into thickest part of ham reaches 130°. (Allow about 3 hours to heat a 10- to 12-pound ham, 2 hours for a 6- to 8-pound ham, 1¾ hours for a 4- to 5-pound ham.)

To prepare topping, combine pineapple, marmalade, cornstarch, vinegar, prepared mustard and coconut in a saucepan. Mix. Heat, stirring constantly, until mixture thickens. Thirty minutes before the end of baking time turn oven to 375°. Fifteen minutes before the end of baking time, spoon fruit mixture over top of ham and sprinkle remaining coconut over fruit topping. Return to oven to finish heating. Arrange on a serving platter. If desired, surround with assorted fresh fruits and mint. Allow 4 servings per pound of ham.

CURRIED RICE

1 c. rice
3 T. butter or margarine, melted
⅓ c. chopped onion
3 T. minced parsley
3 bouillon cubes
2½ c. boiling water
1½ t. curry powder
   Pinch of thyme

Add rice to melted butter and cook over medium heat, stirring frequently for 10 to 15 minutes or until rice turns a light brown. Add onions and parsley. Cook until onion softens. Dissolve bouillon cubes in boiling water. Add bouillon, curry powder and thyme to the rice. Mix well. Cover. Cook over low heat about 20 minutes or until rice is tender and liquid is absorbed. Stir occasionally.

GRAPES ALOHA

2 T. light brown sugar
   Dash of nutmeg
1 c. dairy sour cream
2 c. seedless green grapes
   Fresh pineapple, peeled and sliced

In a small bowl gently blend brown sugar and nutmeg into sour cream. Fold in grapes. Chill. Core and chill pineapple.

To serve, place pineapple slices on chilled dessert plates and cut into bite-sized pieces, but leave intact. Top with ¼ cup grape mixture. If desired, garnish with rings of pineapple.

PINEAPPLE-APRICOT BARS

1 c. margarine	1 jar pineapple jam
1 c. powdered sugar	4 egg whites
4 egg yolks	1 c. sugar
2 c. flour	1 c. coconut
1 jar apricot jam	

Mix margarine and sugar well. Slowly add egg yolks and flour. Pat in 2 cake pans. Bake at 350° for 15 minutes or until brown. Cool, then spread jam on mixture. Beat egg whites until stiff. Add sugar slowly. Add coconut. Put over jam. Bake at 350° for 20 minutes. Cut into bars.

Mrs. Melvin Medema

CASSEROLE PARTY

One of the easiest picnics is the bring-your-own covered dish suppers. Insulated bags and containers will bring casseroles made at home piping hot to the picnic site.

VEGETABLE CASSEROLE

2 c. cooked green beans	2 T. onion, chopped
1½ c. whole kernel corn	1½ t. salt
	1 t. sugar
2¼ c. tomatoes	¼ t. paprika
½ c. butter	Dash of pepper
¼ c. flour	½ c. grated cheese

Place half of the green beans in a buttered casserole. Place corn on beans and arrange tomatoes over the corn, saving the juice. Cover with green beans. Melt butter in a saucepan, blend in flour. Add juice of tomatoes, stirring until thickened. Add onion and seasonings; pour sauce over vegetables. Sprinkle cheese over top. Bake at 400° for 30 minutes. Serve with a garnish of crisp broiled bacon over the top.

Mrs. C. P. Curtis

> Chicken leftovers make delicious hot sandwiches, pot pies and can be added to soups.

FRANKFURTER CASSEROLE

1 lb. frankfurters
2 potatoes, diced
1 8-oz. can tomato sauce
1 small green pepper, chopped
1 small can mushrooms

Cut frankfurters into ½-inch pieces. Boil the potatoes for 2 minutes, drain and put into casserole. Add remaining ingredients and mix just enough to distribute the sauce. Cover casserole and bake in 350° oven about 1 hour.

Marcella Borkowski

PICNIC CASSEROLE

8 ozs. medium-size noodles
1 lb. ground beef
3 T. margarine
2 8-oz. cans tomato sauce
1 c. cottage cheese
8 ozs. cream cheese
½ c. sour cream
½ c. green onions, chopped
1 T. green pepper, chopped
2 T. melted butter or margarine

Cook noodles, rinse and drain. Brown meat in the 3 tablespoons margarine. Stir in tomato sauce. Combine cottage cheese, cream cheese, sour cream, onions and pepper and heat.

Spread half of the noodles in a 2-quart baking dish. Build layers of cheese, meat and noodles until all is used or baking dish is filled. Pour the 2 tablespoons melted butter over top and bake in a 350° oven for 30 minutes. Serves 6 to 8.

Dorothy Brewer

HOT FRUIT CASSEROLE

1 large can pineapple
1 large can peaches
1 large can apricots
1 large can dark cherries, pitted

SAUCE

2 T. flour	1 stick butter
¼ c. sugar	1 c. sherry

Drain all fruit thoroughly. Make sauce in a double boiler. Place fruit in a casserole. Pour sauce over fruit. Marinate overnight. Heat until bubbly in a 350° oven.

Voncille W. Dean

PORK CHOPS AND WILD RICE

½ c. wild rice	½ c. water or tomato juice
1 t. salt	
6 pork chops	

Wash the rice with several rinsings, then cook rice and salt 15 minutes. Season and brown pork chops and place in a casserole dish. Place a thick slice of onion, tomato and green pepper on each chop. Add water or tomato juice. Spoon rice over the chops. Cover and bake in a 350° oven 2 hours.

Mrs. George V. Nelson

SOUTHERN CHICKEN PIE

1 large fryer or stewing-size chicken
1 small onion, chopped fine
2 center stalks celery, chopped fine
2 hard-cooked eggs
2 T. flour
1 c. milk
2 c. chicken broth
  Pastry dough for 2 piecrusts

Boil and bone chicken. Roll pastry dough as for piecrust. Cut in strips and place in bottom of 9 x 13-inch baking dish. Reserve enough to strip over top. Lay chicken pieces over pastry strips. Sprinkle chopped eggs, celery and onion over chicken. Mix flour, milk and broth, and pour over chicken. Then lay pastry strips over all. Bake 30 to 40 minutes in 350° oven.

Clara Golden

RAW APPLE CAKE

For pure enchantment when days are warm,
Unique, unequalled, as summer's charm,
No oven miracle you can bake
Is more appealing than apple cake.

Sweeter than breezes in apple boughs,
More "country" than pastures and placid cows,
Light as a hummingbird's flower flight,
Raw apple cake is pure delight.

D. A. Hoover

RAW APPLE CAKE

4 c. peeled,   1½ t. baking soda
  sliced apples   2 eggs, beaten
2 c. flour   2 t. cinnamon
2 c. sugar   ¾ c. oil
1 t. salt   2 t. vanilla

Mix sugar and apples in a large mixing bowl. Set aside for a few minutes. Mix dry ingredients with apples. Add eggs, oil and vanilla. Mix thoroughly. Pour in a greased 9 x 13-inch pan. Bake 50 minutes in a 350° oven. Top with a favorite frosting.

Golde Hoover

DEVILED MACARONI

1 8-oz. pkg. elbow macaroni,
  cooked and drained
1 10½-oz. can cream of mushroom soup
¼ c. milk
2 T. melted butter
1 c. grated sharp cheese
1 t. onion salt
¼ t. pepper
¼ c. diced pimiento
2 t. prepared mustard
4 hard-cooked eggs, sliced
¼ c. dry bread crumbs

Combine macaroni, soup, milk, cheese, pimiento and seasonings. Spoon half of this mixture into a buttered casserole. Add a layer of sliced eggs. Top with remaining mixture. Mix bread crumbs with butter. Sprinkle over casserole. Bake 40 minutes at 350°. Garnish with sliced eggs. Makes 6 servings.

Lloyd C. Schupbach

PAUL BUNYAN SUGAR COOKIES

⅔ c. shortening   2 c. sifted
¾ c. sugar   all-purpose flour
1 egg   1½ t. baking powder
1½ t. vanilla   ¼ t. salt
4 t. milk

Cream together shortening, sugar, egg and vanilla until light and fluffy. Stir in milk. Sift together dry ingredients. Stir into creamed mixture, blending well.

Divide dough in half. Chill 1 hour. On a lightly floured surface, roll ⅛- to ¼-inch thick. Cut with coffee can lid of canister. Sprinkle tops with sugar. In the center of each cookie place 3 big seeded raisins. Place cookies 1 inch apart on a lightly greased cookie sheet. Bake at 375° about 10 minutes or until lightly browned. Cool slightly and remove from pan. Makes about 5 to 10 five-inch cookies.

Note: If cookies are rolled to ¼ inch, do not divide dough in half.

Carole A. Davis

TAILGATE BUFFET

For a more elaborate picnic, the tailgate of a station wagon makes a table for a handsome buffet.

ROLLED RIB ROAST

Bind one 6- to 8-pound rolled rib roast with a heavy string or butcher's cord. Place on spit, securing with prongs. Turn spit constantly on a low to medium fire. Baste with a sauce and juices from meat. Barbecue meat until it is fork tender and has reached the desired degree of doneness. For rare meat, roast 30 minutes per pound, for medium, 34 minutes per pound, for well done, 40 minutes per pound. Cool before carving.

FRENCH POTATO SALAD

2 lbs. boiled potatoes, peeled and sliced
2 T. dry white vermouth
2 T. chicken bouillon
½ c. vinaigrette
2 T. minced scallions
3 T. minced parsley

In a large mixing bowl, toss potatoes gently with the vermouth and bouillon. After liquid has been absorbed, toss with remaining ingredients.

Mrs. Chester Neils

SQUASH CASSEROLE

1 lb. summer squash	1 c. bread crumbs
2 onions, sliced	¼ c. milk
1 t. sugar	1 c. grated cheese
1 egg	½ stick margarine
Salt and pepper to taste	

Cook squash and onions in salted water until tender. Drain. Beat until light. Add remaining ingredients, reserving a third of the cheese and crumbs for the top layer. Bake at 350° until cheese has melted and top is lightly browned.

Bernice Wilkey

QUICHE LORRAINE

1 9-inch pie shell
8 bacon slices, diced
½ c. chopped green onions and tops
6 eggs, beaten
1 t. onion salt
1 c. shredded Swiss cheese
2 c. light cream

Line pie pan with pie shell. Trim edge and flute. Brown bacon lightly. Drain off excess fat. Add onions and cook until bacon is golden brown. Cool slightly. Combine eggs, cheese and onion salt. Stir in bacon mixture. Add cream and blend well. Pour into pie shell. Bake in preheated 375° oven 30 to 35 minutes or until golden brown. Serve hot.

CARROT CASSEROLE

1 10½-oz. can condensed cream of celery soup
⅓ c. milk
2 10-oz. pkgs. frozen carrots, thawed
1 c. chow mein noodles

Combine first 2 ingredients. Put half of carrots in a 1½-quart casserole dish. Cover with half of soup mixture and half of chow mein noodles; repeat. Cover. Bake in a moderate oven for 25 minutes. Uncover and bake 10 more minutes.

Mrs. J. R. Ronald

APPLE UPSIDE-DOWN CAKE

2 T. butter or margarine
½ c. brown sugar, packed
1¼ c. canned unsweetened apple slices, drained
1 t. cinnamon
1 1-layer pkg. yellow cake mix
Pecan halves

In a 9-inch baking pan melt butter over low heat, then sprinkle brown sugar over butter. Add fruits and nuts. Sprinkle cinnamon over all. Prepare cake mix according to directions. Spread over fruit. Bake 55 minutes in a preheated 350° oven or until done. Cool in pan 5 minutes. Remove from pan. Serve.

Mrs. Ralph W. Visscher

BARBECUED BRISKET

1 whole beef brisket
1 large onion
1 bay leaf
16 whole cloves
1 clove garlic, halved

Cook above ingredients in pot covered with water for 4 hours. Refrigerate meat overnight after removing from the water.

SAUCE

4 T. brown sugar   2 T. Worcestershire
4 t. dry mustard   sauce
2 c. catsup

Mix together. Slice cold meat thinly. Stand up in a casserole dish. Pour sauce over meat. Put meat in a 325° oven about 40 minutes.

Charlotte W. Gagalski

BLACK WALNUT CAKE

½ c. butter
1½ c. sugar
1 t. baking powder
2 c. flour
¾ c. cold water
1 c. chopped black walnuts
4 egg whites, beaten

Cream butter and gradually add the sugar, creaming until light and fluffy. Sift together the baking powder and flour, add it alternately with the water to the creamed mixture. Carefully fold in the nuts and then the egg whites. Bake in two 8-inch layer cake pans for 30 to 35 minutes at 350°. Frost with a walnut frosting.

Donna J. Vossler

CHUCK WAGON CHOW

BARBECUED RIBS

3 lbs. country-style pork spareribs
⅓ c. orange marmalade
¼ c. lemon juice
¼ c. soy sauce
1 clove garlic, minced
2 t. cornstarch
2 T. water
  Salt and pepper

On a large double thickness of heavy-duty aluminum foil place the spareribs in a single layer. Season lightly with salt and pepper. Fold the foil over the ribs and seal at edge and ends with a double fold. Place on grill about 4 inches from the coals and cook 45 minutes, turning once.

Mix the orange marmalade, lemon juice, soy sauce and garlic. Mix cornstarch and water. Add to sauce and cook until thickened, stirring constantly. Remove foil packet of ribs from the grill and open. Place ribs on grill or in grill basket. Spoon sauce on each piece and broil 5 minutes longer.

Doc Kingsley

CHILI BEANS

1 lb. pink beans
2 medium-sized onions, chopped
1 or 2 cloves garlic, minced
3 T. bacon fat
¼ t. cumin seed
1 lb. ground beef
1 8-oz. can Spanish-style tomato sauce
1 T. chili powder
  Salt to taste

Soak beans for 3 hours. Bring to a boil. Sauté onion and garlic in bacon fat until limp and golden. Add meat and cook, stirring with a fork until meat has lost its red color. Add meat mixture and remaining ingredients to the beans. Cover and cook slowly for about 3 hours or until beans are tender. Stir occasionally, adding more water during cooking if necessary. The sauce will be a little thick.

Joy Belle Burgess

BAR-B-QUE BEEF

1½ lbs. beef, cubed
  1 T. shortening
1½ c. water
  1 small onion (or 1 T. onion flakes)
  ½ c. celery, diced
  ⅓ c. green pepper, diced
  1 c. catsup
  ¼ c. brown sugar
  2 T. vinegar
  2 T. Worcestershire sauce
  1 t. chili powder
1½ t. salt

Put shortening, cubed beef, water, onion, celery and green pepper in a skillet. Cook at low temperature until done. Break apart with fork. Mix catsup, brown sugar, vinegar, Worcestershire sauce, chili powder and salt. Add to cooked meat. Simmer 20 to 30 minutes. Serve hot on buns. Makes 16 to 20 servings. Beef may be frozen if made ahead.

Mrs. Gilbert Laabs

SOURDOUGH BISCUITS

1 c. sourdough starter	1 egg
	1 T. shortening
¼ t. baking soda	Flour

Mix all ingredients with enough flour to make kneadable dough. Roll flat on a floured strip of aluminum foil. Cut into biscuits. Allow to raise 1 hour or more. Set biscuits in a greased skillet or Dutch oven and bake until golden brown.

SOURDOUGH STARTER

2 c. flour
2 c. warm water or milk
1 yeast cake

Mix above ingredients well. Put in a warm place overnight. Use only glass or earthenware containers. Starter must be kept in a cool place or frozen.

SPICED PEACHES

3½ c. canned peach halves (save juice)
6 inches stick cinnamon
1 t. cloves
1 T. vinegar

In a large saucepan, combine all ingredients including juice. Heat until mixture boils. Simmer 5 minutes. Chill overnight. Drain before serving.

Mrs. T. A. Naylor

HAPPINESS . . . WESTERN STYLE

Happiness is spending
Some time out of doors
With a gentle wind tossing your hair.
It's a ride...it's a walk...
A "back home" kind of talk...
It's a western bill of fare.

It's a ready smile,
A neighborly style
That is helpful in so many ways.
It's a barbecue treat
As delicious to eat
As the food of the chuck wagon days.

It's barbecued beef
With oven-baked beans
And sourdough biscuits served hot...
Spiced peaches to try
And a cobbler pie
With black coffee served from the pot.

Alice Leedy Mason

RANCH-STYLE BAKED BEANS

2 T. butter or margarine
1 lb. ground chuck or round steak
1 envelope onion soup mix
1 c. catsup
½ c. cold water
2 1-lb. cans pork and beans
in tomato sauce
1 1-lb. can red kidney beans, drained
2 T. prepared mustard
2 t. cider vinegar

Preheat oven to 400°. In a large skillet melt butter and brown meat. Stir in remaining ingredients. Pour into a 2½-quart casserole or bean pot. Bake 30 to 40 minutes until hot and bubbly. Serves 8 to 10.

Mrs. Loren M. Smith

CHERRY COBBLER

½ c. sugar
1 to 2 T. cornstarch
1 can (1 pound, 4 ounces) sour cherries
1 T. butter
¼ t. cinnamon

Combine sugar, cornstarch and juice from cherries. Stir and boil 1 minute. Add remaining ingredients and mix. Pour into a 1½-quart baking dish.

1 c. sifted flour	½ t. salt
2 t. baking powder	3 T. butter
1 T. sugar	½ c. milk

Mix and sift flour, baking powder, sugar and salt. Cut in butter as for biscuits. Add milk and mix until dry ingredients are moistened. Drop by spoonsful on cherries. Bake in a preheated 400° oven about 30 minutes.

Mrs. B. L. Nelson

APPLE BROWN BETTY

3 c. sliced tart apples
1½ c. coarse bread crumbs or graham crackers
¼ c. butter or margarine, melted
1 c. brown sugar
½ t. cinnamon or nutmeg
½ c. water

Mix apples, crumbs, butter and sugar in a 10 x 6 x 2-inch baking pan. Sprinkle with cinnamon or nutmeg. Over all pour the water. Bake at 325° for 45 to 50 minutes. Serve with whipped cream or hard sauce. Serves 6.

Mrs. R. Heykoop

WESTERN CAKE

1 c. shortening	1 t. vanilla
3 c. sugar	2 t. lemon extract
5 eggs	1 t. baking powder
1 c. sweet milk	3 c. flour

Cream together the shortening and sugar. Add the eggs, one at a time, then the remaining ingredients. Mix well. Pour into a tube pan and bake at 325° for 1 hour, then turn oven down to 300° and bake for 30 more minutes. Do not open oven until time to remove the cake. Cool. No icing is needed.

Mrs. Norman Gregory

CREAMY SHRIMP DIP

1 10-oz. can frozen condensed cream of
   shrimp soup, thawed
1 8-oz. pkg. cream cheese, softened
2 T. chopped green onion
1 t. lemon juice
¼ t. curry powder
   Dash of garlic powder
4 drops hot pepper sauce

Gradually blend soup and other ingredients with an electric mixer or rotary beater. Do not overbeat or dip will be too thin. Chill. Serve with raw vegetable sticks. Makes about 2 cups.

FRENCH FRIES IN A POKE

Place partially thawed French fries on a large square of heavy-duty aluminum foil. Sprinkle with salt and pepper. Gather foil up around them, partially closing at top, but leaving room for steam to escape. Place on the grate over fire and heat, shaking the package occasionally for 15 minutes or until hot to the touch.

SAVORY OUTDOOR BAKED FISH

Scale and clean fish, leaving whole or cut into fillets or steaks. Place fish on individual sheets of heavy-duty foil and brush with oil or melted butter. Sprinkle with salt, pepper and lemon juice. Top each fish with a teaspoonful of chopped tomato or pimiento garnished with lemon slices. Bring foil up over fish and seal with a double fold. Seal ends. Place on grate over a medium-hot fire and bake 10 minutes on a side for a small 1- to 1½-pound fish, 15 minutes on a side for 2- to 3-pound fish and about 20 minutes on a side for 4- to 5-pound fish. Open foil and test with a fork. Fish is done when it flakes. Also serve the delicious juice that forms in the package.

FISH BAKE

Fish are at their best cooked just minutes out of the water, so have this fish bake in mind before you leave home and bring along an insulated picnic cooler stocked with the things you'll need to round out the feast.

PICNIC GREEN PEA SOUP

2 T. chopped onion
¼ c. sliced celery
1 T. butter or margarine
1 11¼-oz. can condensed green pea soup
1 soup can of water
½ c. chopped canned tomatoes
   Thyme croutons

Cook onion and celery in butter until tender. Blend in soup; gradually add water and tomatoes. Heat, stirring occasionally. Garnish with croutons. Makes 2 to 3 servings.

Thyme croutons: In a skillet, brown 1 slice of white bread, cut into cubes in 2 tablespoons butter or margarine, stir constantly. Add dash of crushed thyme.

LEMON CAKE

1 19-oz. pkg. yellow cake mix
1 lemon, grated rind and juice
¾ c. sugar
½ c. melted butter

Prepare cake mix according to package directions, adding 1 teaspoon of grated rind. Turn into a 13 x 9 x 2-inch pan. Combine sugar with remaining rind and sprinkle on surface of cake. Combine 1 tablespoon lemon juice and the butter. Sprinkle over sugar. Bake at 350° for 25 to 30 minutes. Cake will have a crispy lemon-flavored top. Cool, leave cake in pan and wrap in foil to carry to cookout. If the day is cool, warm over the coals before serving. Cut in squares.

Note: Cake can also be baked in 2 9-inch round baking pans.

 # CLAMBAKE

You don't have to live at the seashore to have a clambake. Here are two methods to use, one for the beach and another for the backyard.

LEMONADE TEA

Prepare 1 6-ounce can frozen lemonade. Add to 1 quart of iced tea. Sweeten if desired. Pour tea over ice cubes. Serve.

BACKYARD CLAMBAKE

On a 24-inch piece of heavy-duty aluminum foil place 1 large frozen lobster tail, 1 chicken leg, 6 clams, 1 ear of corn (silk removed), 1 scrubbed potato, 1 onion and ½ cup clam juice. Bring up sides of foil and seal with a double fold. Double-fold ends. Place bundle, seam side down, on a second sheet of heavy-duty foil. Wrap and seal with a double fold. Place on grill 4 inches from coals. Cook 1 hour, turning every 15 minutes. Serve with melted butter and lemon. Each bundle serves one.

CLAM CHOWDER

2 10½-oz. cans minced clams, drained
  (save liquid)
4 slices bacon, finely diced
2 medium onions, sliced
4 medium potatoes, peeled and diced
2 c. milk
  Salt and pepper to taste
  Chowder crackers

Add enough water to the clam liquid to make 2 cups. Cook bacon in a large kettle until crisp. Drain all fat except for 2 tablespoons. Add onions and cook, stirring occasionally, until tender. Add clam liquid and potatoes. Cover. Cook until tender. Add clams and heat for 1 or 2 minutes. Add milk and cook until clams and milk are hot. Salt and pepper to taste. Serve with crisp crackers. Serves 4 to 6.

SEASHORE CLAMBAKE

   Seaweed
20 large baking potatoes, scrubbed
20 ears of corn
10 broiling chickens, halved
 5 lobsters
10 qts. soft-shell clams
   Butter, melted

For a clambake for 20 people, dig a pit about 4 x 2 x 4½-feet deep. Line the pit with a layer of dry rocks about the size of a small head of cabbage. Cover with fire wood. Light the fire, then add alternate layers of stones and wood until pile burns down to coals at least 1 foot deep. Remove embers and cover rocks with seaweed. Spread clams over seaweed. Cover with another layer of seaweed. Add lobsters. Cover again with seaweed. Add chickens which have been wrapped in foil with seasonings. Again cover with seaweed. Add a layer of corn and potatoes, each wrapped in foil. Then a thick layer of seaweed is added as well as coals and hot rocks and a final layer of seaweed. Finally, spread a tarpaulin or wet canvas over the top. Fasten around the edges securely. Cook an hour or longer. Remove canvas and seaweed. Serve clams, lobsters and corn with melted butter.

> Keep clambake desserts simple. Chill watermelon in a bucket of ice. Take along firm fresh fruit such as nectarines, peaches, pears.

CHOCOLATE OATMEAL COOKIES

1 c. white sugar
1 c. brown sugar
1 stick butter
½ c. milk
1 6-oz. pkg. chocolate bits
2 c. quick-cooking rolled oats
½ c. finely chopped pecans or walnuts

Cook sugars, butter and milk. Bring to a boil and boil 2 minutes. Remove from heat and add remaining ingredients. Mix well. Let stand about 10 minutes, then drop from teaspoon on greased cookie sheet or waxed paper. Makes 65 cookies.

Maysie Newsom

SKIPPER'S SHORTCAKE

3 T. chopped onion 1½ c. canned fish
2 T. fat Salt and pepper
4 T. flour to taste
2 c. milk Cornbread
⅓ c. grated cheese

Cook onion in the fat until tender. Blend in flour. Slowly add milk, stirring constantly. Cook until thick. Add cheese and fish. Salt and pepper to taste. Heat, stirring occasionally. Serve on cornbread.

Martha Stevenson

CLAM FRITTERS

18 medium clams 1½ t. baking powder
1 egg Pepper and salt
¾ c. flour

Open and grind up the clams. Pick out the meat. Beat the egg into the clams and add flour. Blend together until smooth. Add baking powder. Pepper and salt well.

If there is too much flour use a little clam juice to thin batter. Fry in iron skillet with liberal amount of cooking oil. Fry on both sides until golden brown. Makes about 15 fritters.

Mrs. A. Freeman Endicott

TOMATOES LUTECE

8 large peeled tomatoes
¼ c. chopped parsley
1 crushed garlic clove
1 t. salt
1 t. sugar
¼ t. pepper
¼ c. salad oil
2 T. vinegar
1 t. prepared mustard

Slice tomatoes into ½-inch-thick slices and place in a shallow serving dish. Combine remaining ingredients in a small jar. Cover. Shake well. Pour over tomatoes, cover lightly and allow to stand at least 20 minutes before serving.

Mrs. Kenneth B. Webb

COOKING AFLOAT

Mealtimes can be happy times afloat, be it a cruise, a race, a weekend outing or a day on the water. With limited accommodations, shortcut dishes which can be made in a saucepan or a skillet are a must.

NEPTUNE STEW

6 ozs. crabmeat 2 T. flour
6 ozs. lobster 1½ t. salt
6 ozs. oysters Dash of tabasco
3 ozs. clams 2½ T. cold water
3 ozs. scallops

Combine flour, salt, tabasco and water. Stir into seafood. Add ¼ cup butter. Simmer over low heat until sides of seafood begin to curl. Scald 3 cups milk and 1 cup light cream. Mix milk and seafood mixture and simmer 1 hour.

Louise Hanicker

SAILORS' STROGANOFF

1 lb. hamburger
Chopped onion
1 can cream of chicken soup
1 c. sour cream

Brown hamburger and onion in a skillet. Add soup and simmer 1 hour. Add sour cream just before serving. Serve over rice or noodles.

Mrs. Melvin D. Heckt

FRIED CHICKEN DELUXE

3 T. flour 1 can cream of
1 t. salt mushroom soup
½ t. pepper 3 T. corn oil
1 cut-up fryer

Heat corn oil in a skillet. Roll chicken in flour, salt and pepper. Brown on both sides in the oil. Then add soup and 2 cans of water. Simmer 40 minutes until tender.

Dot Curry

SAUSAGE SUPPER FOR TWO

Place 6 sausages in a skillet. Add water to partially cover. Add 6 or 8 small peeled potatoes and 2 carrots cut lengthwise. Cover dish and cook slowly. As water boils down add more if necessary. Cook about ½ hour. Brown sausage at last without uncovering.

Mrs. Hugh Morenz

ONE-PAN PORK CHOPS

For each serving:

Brown one pork chop on both sides. Put a thick slice of onion on top of each pork chop. Put a ring of green pepper on top of onion. Put one tablespoon raw rice (not instant) inside green pepper ring. Moisten rice with tomato juice. Top with one whole canned tomato.

Dice several carrots and a few stalks of celery, add to chops in skillet, pour remaining canned tomatoes and juice over all, cover tightly and allow to simmer for at least 45 minutes. (Extra juice may be added as needed.)

Note: Use a heavy skillet with a tight lid.

Leona Krefting

MEATBALL SKILLET SUPPER

¼ c. chopped onion	½ t. pepper
1 T. margarine	2 T. flour
1 lb. hamburger	1 egg
1½ t. salt	¼ c. light cream

Cook onion in margarine until tender but not brown. Combine meat and seasoning and beat well. Beat in flour, then egg. Gradually beat in cream. Add onion. (This should be light and fluffy.) Form into 1-inch meatballs and brown lightly in a little more butter. Shake skillet to turn balls. Cook with the following vegetables:

```
 6 to 10 small potatoes, cut in small chunks
12 small carrots, quartered
 5 green onions
 2 c. peas (optional)
 1 can condensed consommé
```
Cook for 20 minutes or until done.

Dot Curry

CORN CHOWDER

```
5 slices bacon
1 onion, sliced thin and separated
1 17-oz. can cream corn
  Salt and dash of pepper
2 medium potatoes, diced
½ c. water
1 c. milk
1 c. cream
```

Cook bacon crisp, crumble. Save 3 tablespoons fat. Cook onions in fat until light brown. Add potatoes and water. Cook 10 minutes. Add remaining ingredients and heat.

Jane F. Prudden

ONE-DISH MEAT LOAF MEAL

2 lbs. ground beef	½ c. bread crumbs
½ c. tomato sauce	1 t. salt
1 small onion	⅛ t. pepper
(optional)	1 egg

Mix together and place in a baking dish.

SAUCE

½ c. tomato sauce	2 T. sugar
1 c. water	2 T. vinegar
2 T. prepared	4 potatoes, peeled
mustard	4 carrots

Mix first 5 ingredients together. Place potatoes and carrots around the meat loaf. Pour sauce over mixture and bake at 350° for 1½ hours. Baste occasionally.

Mary Alice Campbell

FRIED CORN

Put 4 tablespoons bacon grease in a skillet. Cut corn from 6 ears of sweet corn into the skillet. Season to taste with salt and pepper. Cover. Cook, stirring to keep corn from burning.

FRIED CABBAGE

Put 4 tablespoons bacon grease in a skillet. Cut up 1 head of cabbage in chunks into the skillet. Add ½ cup water. Season to taste with salt and pepper. Cover. Let simmer.

Ruby Davenport Kish

TROUT FRY

3 pan-sized trout	¼ t. sage
½ c. flour	Salt and pepper
½ c. cornmeal	to taste
1 t. onion powder	1 stick butter
¼ t. garlic powder	¼ c. brandy

Combine flour, cornmeal and seasonings in a bowl. Melt butter in a skillet. Dip trout in the flour-cornmeal-seasonings mixture, coating generously. Drop into sizzling butter and brown well on both sides. Pour brandy directly over trout, simmer and cover with a tight-fitting lid. Continue simmering for 20 more minutes or until fish is flaky. Serves three.

Andrew J. Shafer

43

GOULASH

¾ pkg. spaghetti
1 lb. hamburger
4 slices bacon
1 onion
¼ green pepper
1 medium can tomatoes
  Salt and pepper to taste

Cook spaghetti in boiling water and drain. Fry bacon, onion and pepper until very brown. Add hamburger. When brown add spaghetti and tomatoes. Cook until most of moisture has been absorbed but not dry. Serves 4 to 6.

Mrs. James E. Cole

POTATO OMELET

¼ c. olive oil
1 large onion, minced
1 large potato, peeled and minced
5 large eggs, beaten

Place olive oil in 8- or 10-inch pan over moderate heat. Add onion and potato. Cook slowly, chopping occasionally as they cook, until very soft but not browned. Sprinkle salt over vegetables. Add about ⅓ of the eggs, lift up with spatula at edges and in center to allow moist egg to run under. Add remaining eggs, half at a time. When eggs are firm but still slightly moist (not runny) and golden on bottom, run a spatula under omelet to loosen, then place plate over top and invert pan. Carefully scrape any bits clinging to pan, add another tablespoon olive oil, slide omelet back into pan with moist side down. Continue cooking over moderate heat until golden on the other side.

Edith Pikelny

CHOCOLATE PIE

1 c. sugar
2 eggs
2 T. cocoa
2 heaping T. flour
2 c. boiling water
1 8-inch baked piecrust

Mix thoroughly sugar, cocoa, flour and eggs. Add boiling water a little at a time and mix well. Boil to thicken. Add butter and vanilla to flavor. Do not use milk in place of water. When filling is cool, place in baked piecrust.

Alma Helen Moore

BARBECUED CHEESE POTATOES

4 large potatoes
¼ c. chopped onion
1½ c. milk
1 T. butter
½ t. salt
⅛ t. pepper
1 T. chopped parsley
1 T. catsup
½ t. Worcestershire sauce
  Dash of tabasco
¾ c. processed American cheese, finely diced

Peel potatoes and slice thin. Then combine all ingredients and pour into a heavy skillet or Dutch oven. Cover. Cook over low heat until potatoes are tender, about 1 hour. Serve with grilled beef patties and crisp green salad.

Martha Hendren

UNBAKED CARAMEL COOKIES

2 c. sugar
¾ c. butter
1 5⅓-oz. can evaporated milk
1 3-oz. pkg. instant butterscotch pudding
3½ c. quick-cooking rolled oats

Combine first 3 ingredients in a large saucepan. Bring to a rolling boil, stirring frequently. Remove from heat. Add butterscotch pudding. Mix well. Then add rolled oats. Cool 15 minutes. Drop from teaspoon onto waxed paper or lightly greased cookie sheet. Cool. Roll in flaked coconut if desired. Makes 60 cookies.

Maysie Newsom

SKILLET COOKIES

1 stick butter, melted
1 egg, well beaten
1 c. sugar
1 c. dates, cut fine
2 to 2¾ c. crispy rice cereal
¾ to 1 c. pecans or walnuts
1 t. vanilla

To the melted butter, add egg, sugar and dates. Cook in skillet for approximately 6 minutes, stirring constantly. Remove from heat. Add cereal, nuts and vanilla. Form into 1-inch balls (form the balls loosely) and roll in powdered sugar.

Beth Green

SHRIMP DELIGHT

2 large bags shrimp
1 lb. fresh mushrooms
2 fresh green peppers, cut in strips
1 large Bermuda onion
2 cans cream of mushroom soup, undiluted

In a large skillet melt some butter, adding green pepper strips and onion until cooked. Drain cooked mushrooms and shrimp and put in skillet. Just before serving add soup to mixture. Heat well and serve in patty shells or on rice.

Irene M. Jameson

SALMON CROQUETTES

1 pt. can salmon	1 T. flour
1 pt. milk	1 c. bread crumbs
3 eggs	Pepper, mace or
1 T. butter	nutmeg to taste

Mix well. Shape into small patties. Fry in skillet or deep fry.

Leietta M. Taylor

STEAK ROLLS

6 slices boneless steak
3 slices bacon, halved
3 c. water
½ c. chopped onions
3 T. flour
¾ c. shortening
½ t. salt
⅓ t. pepper

Salt and pepper steak slices on both sides. Spread with bacon slices and cover with onions. Roll slices tightly and tie with string. Flour lightly. Place in pan with well-heated shortening and brown. Mix remaining flour with water to form gravy, and pour over steak slices. Simmer 30 minutes. Serve hot after cutting off strings.

Virginia K. Oliver

POTATO CAKES

4 large potatoes	¼ t. cinnamon
1 medium onion	¼ t. salt
(optional)	¼ c. flour

Grate or grind potatoes and onion. Mix above ingredients together and fry in cooking oil. Makes 12 4-inch cakes.

Mary A. Miller

CAMP DINNERS

The key to camp cooking is simplicity. Choose foods that are easy to prepare. A large covered skillet or Dutch oven is perfect for casseroles, stews and soup. Cook just enough for one meal so leftovers won't be a problem.

HUSH PUPPIES

12 ozs. cornmeal	4 ozs. flour
1 large onion, minced	1 t. baking powder
	1 t. salt
1 T. sugar	1 egg

Sift dry ingredients together. Stir in the unbeaten egg. Add onion. Stir in enough milk to make a heavy, dry batter.

Heat a large amount of vegetable oil in a skillet. Dip a soup spoon into the hot oil and cut the hush puppies to the desired size. Dip the spoon into the hot oil after each cut. Brown and serve.

Mrs. Lloyd Malone

EQUIPMENT CHECKLIST

Knives, forks, spoons	Toaster
	Wooden bowl
Mixing spoon, spatulas	Salt and pepper shakers
Aluminum foil	Can, bottle opener
Ladle	Ice pick
Measuring cup	Ice chest or
Nested saucepans with covers	refrigerator
	Funnel
Skillet	Dishpan and towels
Coffee pot	Eggbeater
Colander	Pot holders
Double boiler	Fire extinguisher

BUSY-DAY STEW

1½ to 2 lbs. round steak, ½-inch thick
    Flour
  4 T. shortening
  8 medium new potatoes, quartered
  4 large carrots
  1 large onion, diced
  1 T. Worcestershire sauce
1½ t. salt
  ½ t. seasoned salt
  ⅛ t. pepper
  ¼ t. oregano

Dredge round steak in flour. Cut into 1½-inch squares and brown in hot fat in a heavy skillet or Dutch oven. Add potatoes, carrots (cut into ½-inch slices), onion and seasonings. Add ½ inch of water, cover tightly and simmer 1 hour or until steak is tender.

VARIATION

For leftover meat and gravy, scrub and cook cut-up vegetables in salted boiling water until tender, approximately 25 minutes. Drain off part of excess water. Add cooked diced meat and gravy and warm thoroughly.

Dorothy Horst

BASIC BISCUIT MIX

This biscuit mix can be used in several different ways.

12 c. flour   ½ c. sugar
½ c. baking powder   2 c. shortening
 2 T. salt

Blend as for pastry. Store in a covered jar.

Biscuits: Add enough milk to form a stiff dough.

Dumplings: Add enough milk or water to form a soft dough.

Pancakes: Add enough milk and 1 beaten egg to form a pouring batter.

Muffins: 2 cups of the biscuit mix, 1 egg and ¾ cup milk makes 6 medium muffins.

Cupcakes: Add a few currants and a little extra sugar to the muffin mix.

Winnifred Elsaesser

VEGETABLE-BEAN SOUP

  ½ lb. ground beef
  1 T. salad oil
  1 c. chopped onion
3½ c. water
  1 envelope vegetable soup mix
  1 c. celery and leaves, cut fine
  1 1-lb. can baked beans in tomato sauce
  1 c. tomato juice

Brown beef and onion in salad oil, then add other ingredients. Cook approximately 20 minutes.

Linda B. Keyes

PANNING VEGETABLES

Vegetables cooked by this method have fresh flavor, bright color, and practically all of their original food value.

Shred or slice vegetable. Heat a small amount of butter or margarine in a heavy pan with a flat bottom over moderate heat. Add vegetable and sprinkle with salt. Stir vegetable so each piece glistens with fat. Add water and cover pan to hold in steam. Cook over low heat until tender. Stir occasionally to prevent sticking. Make 4 to 6 servings at a time.

WILTED LETTUCE

1 T. bacon grease   1 T. sugar
2 T. sour cream   Salt and pepper
1 T. vinegar   to taste

Prepare leaf lettuce. Put bacon grease in a skillet. Add above ingredients. Stir mixture until hot. Pour over lettuce and serve.

Ruby Davenport Kish

BRUSHPILE PORK CHOPS

4 to 6 pork chops
1 c. quick-cooking rice
1 pkg. dehydrated onion soup

Brown pork chops in a little oil, then remove from skillet. Pour in rice. Brown rice in drippings, stirring often. Pour in soup. Mix thoroughly with the rice. Return pork chops to skillet and add enough water to cover the chops. Cover. Cook until pork chops are tender.

Frieda J. Hawes

HOT CHOCOLATE MIX

4 lb. box instant nonfat dry milk
1 lb. box confectioners' sugar
1 lb. box powdered chocolate drink mix
1 11-oz. jar non-dairy cream

Mix all ingredients well. Store in large container.

To make hot chocolate drink, use ⅓ cup dry mix to small cup of hot water or ⅔ cup dry mix to coffee mug.

Mrs. Tommy Cochran

TOMATO RAREBIT

1 10¾-oz. can tomato soup
¼ c. milk
1 c. shredded sharp cheddar cheese

In a saucepan, combine above ingredients. Cook over low heat, stirring often until cheese is melted. Serve over toast. Makes 3 to 4 servings.

S'MORES

Try this do-it-yourself dessert around a campfire or on a winter evening around the fireplace.

2 graham crackers
½ chocolate bar
1 roasted marshmallow

Place chocolate on 1 graham cracker and put roasted marshmallow on chocolate. Top with second cracker. The marshmallow melts the chocolate.

Mrs. Vern Cornwell

SPEEDY SAUSAGE-MACARONI DINNER

2 12-oz. pkgs. fully cooked smoked sausage links
3 15-oz. cans macaroni with cheese sauce
¾ c. finely chopped onion (or sliced green onions)
1½ T. prepared mustard
1 8-oz. pkg. sliced pasteurized process American cheese
2 tomatoes, sliced

Reserve 12 sausage links for top of pan. Cut remaining links diagonally into ¼-inch slices. Combine sliced sausage, macaroni and cheese sauce, onion and mustard in large shallow skillet. Mix. Cover. Bring to serving temperature, stirring carefully several times during heating. Heat remaining sausage links in skillet or hot water as directed on package. Arrange links attractively on top of heated macaroni. Cut American cheese in half diagonally. Garnish top of sausage links with overlapping cheese and tomato slices. Let stand just until cheese softens.

GRAHAM CRACKER BARS

¾ c. butter   2 eggs, beaten
½ c. coconut   1 c. sugar
1 t. vanilla

Cook above ingredients in a double boiler until thick like custard. Cool. Mix with:

2 c. graham crackers, crushed
½ c. nuts
2½ c. miniature marshmallows

Mix well and put in buttered pan. Cool, then cut into squares.

Sister M. Mercedes, S.C.C.

DELICIOUS CHILI

2 lbs. hamburger
½ c. shortening
4 large onions, diced
2 buttons garlic
1½ c. dry kidney beans
4 large chili peppers
1 large can tomatoes
1 T. sugar
1 T. salt
Dash of pepper
3 heaping t. chili powder
2 heaping t. cumin powder

Soak beans and peppers overnight. Cook until medium tender. Remove skins from peppers. Cook meat, onions, garlic in the shortening. Add to the beans. Then add remaining ingredients. Simmer several hours. Serve with salted crackers.

Mrs. Paul E. King

AUTUMN

Now autumn plies her brush in glen and
wood,
To splash her canvases with gold and flame
And redesign those hills where April stood
Before surrendering to winter's claim.
A misty wind blows inland from the sea,
To spin the maple leaves down to the ground
In dizzy swirls . . . a careless symphony
Of tumbling, golden notes of whispered
sound.
Brush back the stars and let the moon hang
low!
Soon will the music change to winter's dirge,
When summer dreams lie buried deep in
snow
And falling leaves and falling snowflakes
merge
Into the hour when hearth-fires glow again,
Like crimson sunsets on the windowpane.

Elmera J. Cartwright

BAKED APPLES

Core apples and fill with a pat of butter and a little cinnamon and sugar. Place each apple on a square of aluminum foil. Gather up foil and twist together. Bake on medium-hot coals, turning occasionally. A medium-sized apple will take about 45 minutes.

HOMEMADE ROLLS

2 pkgs. powdered yeast
¼ c. lukewarm water
6½ c. flour
½ t. salt
3 T. shortening
2 c. lukewarm milk
2 T. sugar

Dissolve yeast in water. Add milk, shortening, sugar, salt and 3 cups of the flour. Mix well. Add remaining flour. Knead on slightly floured board. Put in greased bowl in a warm place and let raise 1 hour. Knead again. Roll and cut in rolls, place on greased baking sheet and let raise again. Bake in a 350° oven until done. Remove from oven and brush tops with butter.

Mrs. Virgie Edwards

DANDY DOUGHNUTS

3½ to 4 c. flour	1 t. vanilla
2 t. cream of tartar	1 T. grated lemon
½ t. salt	rind
½ t. nutmeg	2 eggs, well
3 T. butter or	beaten
margarine	1 t. soda
1 c. sugar	1 c. milk

Sift dry ingredients. Cream butter and sugar. Add vanilla, lemon rind, eggs. Stir until smooth. Dissolve baking soda in the milk. Gradually add to the creamed mixture, alternating with the dry ingredients. Stir well.

Roll out the dough ⅜-inch thick on a floured board. Cut with a doughnut cutter. Allow to stand 20 minutes. Fry in deep fat at 375°. Brown the doughnuts and lift from the kettle with tongs or a fork. Drain on several thicknesses of absorbent paper. The doughnuts may be sugared or glazed if desired.

Minnie Klemme

COOKING WITH FOIL

For a real adventure in eating, cook a whole meal in foil. The packet seals in the juices and the result is delicious.

GRILLED VEGETABLES

For each serving, place a large cabbage leaf on a generous square of heavy-duty aluminum foil. On top of cabbage leaf add a thick slice of onion. Next lay an unpeeled potato sliced lengthwise. On top of the potato add a slice of tomato, green pepper and zucchini squash. Salt and pepper to taste. Dot with butter throughout. Wrap cabbage leaf around all vegetables and fasten with toothpicks. Wrap in foil and seal carefully with a double fold on top. Grill close to coals, about 20 minutes. Open package to test for tenderness. Reseal for longer cooking.

Virginia Kraegenbrink

Use aluminum foil to line your charcoal pit . . . to wrap potatoes for baking . . . as a drip pan under large roasts . . . as a covered container to cook vegetables, heat breads, and then as a "dish" to serve them. And don't forget those disposable foil cooking utensils!

FISH BANQUET

1 1-lb. fish	1 onion, sliced
2 potatoes, peeled	Seasoning to taste
2 slices bacon	

Cut off a 12-inch square of aluminum foil. Lay 1 slice of bacon on foil. Place the clean fish on top of the bacon. Top with second bacon slice. Add potatoes and onion. Season to taste. Wrap food in foil, folding edges and ends over twice. Place upside down on another piece of foil. Seal again. Place in hot ashes or on top of grill away from direct flame. Cook 15 to 20 minutes on each side after packet begins to sizzle. Remove the outer foil and serve.

Linda Harriman

MEAL IN A BUNDLE

2 lbs. lean chuck, cut into 1-inch cubes
6 medium potatoes, peeled and diced
6 T. chopped onions
6 carrots, sliced
½ c. chopped parsley
2 10½-oz. cans condensed mushroom soup
  Salt and pepper to taste
  Tabasco sauce

Divide above ingredients into 6 equal portions. Place each portion on an 18-inch square of heavy-duty aluminum foil. Add a couple dashes of tabasco and 1 tablespoon of water to each portion. Salt and pepper to taste. Bring up corners of foil and twist at top to close bundles. Line grill with heavy-duty aluminum foil and place bundles on grill 2 inches above hot gray coals. Cook 1 hour. Serve right in the foil.

THE PACKET PLAN

The packet plan for charcoal grills
Is really fun to use.
You may decide to try my plan
Or others if you choose.

A tin-foil packet is prepared
And filled with just these four:
One large potato, thickly sliced,
And carrots — two or more.

A pat of hamburger comes next,
One-fourth a pound works fine.
And top it off with onion sliced —
The sweet Bermuda kind.

Then turn your packet oftentimes
While cooking on the grill.
In 30 minutes — maybe more —
It's done, so eat your fill.

A variation that is grand
Calls for a slice of ham,
Raw sweet potatoes thinly sliced,
And canned pineapple rings.

The packet plan is easily made
And, oh, such fun to eat.
The flavors blend while they are grilled
To make a real treat.

Craig E. Sathoff

50

CHICKEN PACKETS

1 broiler fryer, quartered
1 envelope dehydrated onion soup
4 T. butter
1 t. paprika
1 4-oz. can mushrooms, drained
½ c. cream

Rinse chicken, dry and remove small protruding bones. Cut 4 squares of heavy-duty aluminum foil. On each square put 1 teaspoon butter, 1 tablespoon dehydrated soup and ¼ teaspoon paprika. Add chicken. Sprinkle with remaining soup and butter. Add mushrooms and cream to each serving. Bring foil up over the food, sealing edges with a tight double fold. Cook chicken on hot grill until tender, about 45 minutes to 1 hour. Turn chicken every 10 minutes.

STUFFED GREEN PEPPERS

6 medium green peppers
1 15-oz. can chili with meat
1 12-oz. can whole kernel corn, drained
¾ c. catsup
¼ t. tabasco
¾ c. bread crumbs

Slice top of peppers, remove seeds and membranes. Drop into boiling water, cook 5 minutes. Drain and cool. Place each pepper on heavy-duty aluminum foil. Combine remaining ingredients. Mix well. Divide mixture equally and fill each pepper. Wrap foil around peppers. Double fold at top. Place 6 inches above hot gray coals. Cook 30 to 40 minutes.

CHEESE OR GARLIC BREAD

2 T. grated parmesan cheese
  or 1 clove garlic, minced
¼ lb. soft butter
1 loaf French bread

Add cheese or garlic to the soft butter. Mix well. Let stand 1 hour. Slice bread diagonally almost through loaf. Separate the slices slightly and spread both sides with butter mixture. Wrap tightly in aluminum foil. Heat on grill, turning frequently.

HOT HAM AND CHEESE ROLLS

½ lb. boiled ham, cut into ½-inch cubes
½ lb. processed sharp cheese, cut into
  ½-inch cubes
¼ c. chopped onion
½ c. tomato paste
½ c. pimiento-stuffed olives, sliced
2 hard-cooked eggs, coarsely chopped
2 T. mayonnaise
8 to 12 frankfurter rolls, split

Combine meat, cheese, onion, olives and eggs. Blend mayonnaise into tomato paste. Add to meat mixture. Spread in split rolls. Wrap each roll in aluminum foil, twisting ends tightly. Warm over hot coals.

Charlene Myers

PAULSELL BURGERS

Ground steak patties
Green pepper strips
Onion rings
Tomatoes, sliced
American cheese, sliced
Salt and ground pepper
Mustard

Place a ground steak patty on aluminum foil (shape patties ¼-inch thick and 6 inches in diameter). Then place on top of each patty green pepper strips, onion rings, sliced tomatoes and American cheese slice. Season to taste with salt, pepper and mustard. Add another ground steak patty on top. Wrap in foil. Place on outdoor grill. Cook 10 minutes on each side, using low heat. Unwrap and serve with a tossed salad and garlic bread.

Willabelle Lanning Wiley

FOIL-ROASTED POTATOES

Wash potatoes, then brush with salad oil. Wrap in double-thick aluminum foil, overlapping ends. Preheat gas grill. Cook potatoes on hot grill until tender, about 1 hour. Turn potatoes often.

TOPPINGS FOR BAKED POTATOES

Sour cream, chopped parsley and desired
  seasonings
Cream cheese, sour cream and desired
  seasonings
Chopped olives and sour cream
Crumbled, crisp bacon
Sautéed sliced mushrooms
Grated cheddar cheese
Chopped chives
Sautéed chopped onion

Cook frozen vegetables on a grill by removing them from the package, adding dots of butter, a dash of salt and then wrapping them in heavy foil. Turn once while cooking.

DELUXE BROILED SANDWICHES

1 lb. ground beef
½ t. salt
¼ lb. processed American cheese, grated
1 2-oz. can mushroom stems and pieces, drained and chopped
1 t. Worcestershire sauce
1 t. Kitchen Bouquet
4 slices of bread
Melted butter

Combine beef, salt, cheese, mushrooms, Worcestershire sauce and Kitchen Bouquet and mix well. Spread on slices of bread and cut each slice diagonally into 2 pieces. Brush meat with melted butter. Place sandwiches on broiler rack. Place rack so that tops of sandwiches are about 2 inches below flame. Broil about 15 minutes. Yield: 4 servings.

Charlene Myers

TOASTED SANDWICHES

Butter 2 slices of bread. Spread unbuttered side of 1 slice with a favorite sandwich filling. Top with second slice of bread, buttered side up. Put in grill and close securely. Hold grill over medium heat. Turn frequently. Sandwich is done when bread turns a golden brown and filling is warm.

GRILLED SANDWICHES

Spread a slice of bread with a favorite sandwich filling. Top with another slice of bread. Brush bread with butter. Place sandwich between 2 sheets of aluminum foil in a hand grill. Grill over medium heat. Turn frequently. Barbecue until filling is piping hot.

Mrs. C. P. Burnett

BREADS FOR SANDWICHES

Brown	French or Italian bread
Cheese bread	Hamburger buns
Corn bread	Hard rolls
Cracked wheat	Pumpernickel
Date, orange or banana nut	Raisin, cinnamon raisin
Enriched white	Rye
Frankfurter rolls	Whole wheat

SANDWICH SPREAD

6 medium green tomatoes	6 green bell peppers
6 medium onions	1 piece of celery
	Handful of salt

Grind all ingredients together except salt with the fine blade of a food grinder. Mix together. Add salt. Let stand in salt brine 1 hour. Drain well.

DRESSING

5½ c. granulated sugar	1 qt. vinegar
1 t. turmeric	3 heaping T. mustard
	1 c. flour

Mix above ingredients together, then pour over vegetables. Bring to a boil over medium heat, stirring constantly. Cook 15 minutes. Pour into sterilized pint jars and seal.

Mrs. Paul E. King

STUFFED FRANKFURTERS

Cut a long slit lengthwise in frankfurters to make a pocket. Brush with mustard. Fill with a strip of cheddar cheese and 2 tablespoons sauerkraut. Wrap with bacon spiral-fashion. Fasten with toothpicks. Place on grill over hot coals. Grill until bacon is brown and crisp.

VARIATION

Stuff frankfurter with a stick of dill pickle or fruit or drained baked beans.

Virginia Kraegenbrink

TOASTED HAMBURGERS

1 lb. ground beef
2 T. chopped onions
½ c. milk
Salt and pepper to taste
8 slices of bread

Toast bread on one side. Spread other side with butter and then with mustard. Spread on hamburger mixture, covering to edge of bread. Broil.

Mrs. Alton W. Cheney

CAESAR SALAD

Romaine or head lettuce
Parmesan cheese, grated
Juice of 1 lemon
1 t. tarragon vinegar
2 eggs, simmered 1 minute
Freshly ground pepper, salt,
   dry mustard
⅓ c. olive oil
Croutons

Tear chilled romaine or iceberg lettuce into bite-size pieces. Season with freshly ground pepper, salt and dry mustard to taste. Rub sides of wooden salad bowl with split clove of garlic. Add the greens, parmesan cheese, olive oil, lemon juice and tarragon vinegar. Break simmered eggs over greens, toss to coat lettuce thoroughly, then add the croutons.

Patricia L. Rogers

VEGETABLE SALAD

Drain:

1 can French-style green beans
1 can kidney beans
1 can tiny green peas
1 small jar pimientos, chopped

Chop:

4 stalks celery   1 medium onion
1 green pepper

Combine thoroughly:

 1 c. salad oil   1 T. salt
½ c. vinegar   1 t. paprika
 1 c. sugar

Combine dressing with vegetables. Cover and refrigerate overnight or several hours.

Mrs. Kenneth B. Webb

SHRIMP MACARONI SALAD

1 box ring macaroni, cooked
1 6-oz. jar black olives, pitted
1 can shrimp
6 hard-cooked eggs
2 stalks celery, cut up
2 small green onions
2 ozs. Colby cheese, cut up
½ t. onion salt
1 c. mayonnaise

Use half of the olives. Dice all ingredients and toss with the following seasonings to taste: salt, pepper, parsley flakes, seasoned salt, dash of garlic salt and celery salt. Chill for 2 hours. Before serving add the mayonnaise. Garnish with paprika and slices of 1 egg.

Mrs. Leonard Nelson

WALDORF SALAD

3 c. diced, unpeeled red apples
1 c. diced celery
½ c. mayonnaise
½ c. walnut pieces
  Salad greens
  Cinnamon

Combine apples, celery and mayonnaise to moisten. Serve on salad greens, sprinkle with walnuts and cinnamon.

Edith Pikelny

COTTAGE CHEESE POTATO SALAD

¼ c. dairy sour cream
2 T. Italian dressing
2 c. peeled, diced, cooked potatoes
2 hard-cooked eggs, chopped
2 c. cottage cheese
½ c. sliced celery
⅓ c. chopped ripe olives
⅓ c. sliced radishes
⅓ c. chopped green onions
½ t. salt

In a large bowl blend together sour cream and dressing. Add potatoes and eggs and allow to marinate while preparing remaining ingredients. Add cottage cheese, celery, olives, radishes, onions and salt to potatoes. Mix well. Pack into 4½-cup ring mold. Refrigerate several hours. When ready to serve, unmold onto salad greens. Fill center with vegetable stick relishes if desired.

COLE SLAW IMPERIAL

1 small head cabbage, shredded
1 large carrot, shredded
1 large apple, diced
½ c. small marshmallows, diced
½ c. chopped walnuts (optional)
½ c. mayonnaise or salad dressing
1 T. sugar
3 T. vinegar

Mix cabbage, carrot, apple, marshmallows and nuts. Mix mayonnaise, sugar and vinegar. Pour mayonnaise mixture over cabbage mixture. Stir. Serves 6 to 8.

Margaret Seyfried

CARROT SALAD

1 c. boiled carrots, chopped fine
2 T. chopped sweet pickles
1 c. celery, cut fine
2 hard-boiled eggs, chopped fine
1 c. mayonnaise
1 small onion

Mix all ingredients together. Serve on lettuce leaves with a dash of paprika.

Mrs. J. D. O'Neill

BAKED SEAFOOD SALAD

6 T. chopped green pepper
3 T. chopped onion
1 c. diced celery
1 5½-oz. can crabmeat
1 4½-oz. can shrimp
¾ c. mayonnaise
¼ t. salt
¼ t. pepper
½ t. Worcestershire sauce
¾ c. crushed potato chips

Combine all ingredients except potato chips and mix thoroughly. Turn into a greased quart casserole. Sprinkle with crushed potato chips. Bake in a 350° oven until thoroughly heated, about 30 minutes.

Mrs. Gordon O'Toole

BROCCOLI SALAD

1 pkg. chopped frozen broccoli
¾ c. sliced green olives
1 small onion, chopped
3 hard-cooked eggs, chopped
½ c. mayonnaise

Cook broccoli according to package directions. Drain and cool. Add remaining ingredients.

Note: This salad can be made a day ahead.

Mrs. Kenneth L. Gray

CRUNCHY CHICKEN SALAD

1 c. raw carrots, shredded
¼ c. onion, minced
1 c. celery, diced
1 c. cooked chicken, diced
½ c. salad dressing, thinned with cream
1 T. pickle relish
1 can shoestring potatoes

Combine vegetables with dressing and relish. Add chicken and potatoes just before serving. Tuna may be substituted for chicken if desired.

Mrs. Everett M. Smith

CALICO BEAN SALAD

2 c. canned green beans
2 c. canned wax beans
2 c. canned kidney beans
1 can garbanzos
¾ c. sugar
⅔ c. vinegar
⅓ c. salad oil
　 Salt
½ large onion, sliced in rings

Drain beans, combine in bowl and add ½ c. thinly sliced green pepper. Combine rest of ingredients and shake in a jar.

Prepare salad in morning if possible, and serve at night. Stir several times during day. Refrigerate. Serves 6.

Evelyn M. Samrady

OVERNIGHT LETTUCE SALAD

1 head lettuce, cut in small pieces
½ bunch celery, sliced
1 or 2 3-oz. cans water chestnuts, sliced
1 green pepper, cut in small pieces
1 or 2 pkgs. frozen peas, thawed
　 Sweet onions, sliced
2 c. mayonnaise
1 or 2 T. granulated sugar
2 to 4 T. grated parmesan cheese

Prepare this salad in layers. Spread mayonnaise on top, then sprinkle with sugar and then with cheese. Store overnight in refrigerator. Salad mixes as it is served.

Helen Reynolds

DESSERT SALAD

1 large can fruit cocktail, drained
1 15-oz. can chunk pineapple, drained
½ bag miniature marshmallows
⅓ c. coconut, shredded
3 T. sour cream
　 Chopped walnuts to taste

Add marshmallows, coconut and walnuts to fruit. Mix sour cream into the mixture and let stand 1 to 2 hours in the refrigerator.

Mrs. Norman Tice

MAKE-AHEAD CABBAGE SALAD

10 c. shredded cabbage
2 c. shredded carrots
1 green pepper, minced
1 small onion, minced

Mix the vegetables together and then toss with the following dressing. Put in a cool place so vegetables will stay crisp. Keep covered in refrigerator.

DRESSING

1 T. unflavored gelatin
1 c. vinegar
1½ c. white sugar
1 t. celery seed
1 t. salt
¼ t. pepper
1 c. salad oil

Soften gelatin in a little cold water. Heat vinegar and sugar until sugar dissolves. Add seasonings. Stir into gelatin. Beat in the salad oil.

Edna Thompson

MOTHER'S SALAD DRESSING

3 eggs
1 c. white sugar
Dash of pepper
1 c. white vinegar (plus 1 cup [½ vinegar, ½ water] to make a paste with dry ingredients)
2 t. dry mustard
4 heaping T. flour
½ t. salt
1½ c. boiling water

Beat eggs and sugar. Then make a paste with dry ingredients and add to egg mixture. Add the 1 cup of vinegar and 1½ cups boiling water. Cook in a double boiler until thick. Place in sealer and refrigerate.

If a thinner consistency is desired, thin with milk or cream as needed.

Lynda Malleau

SOUR CREAM-BLUE CHEESE DRESSING

½ c. crumbled blue cheese
½ t. salt
⅛ t. pepper
1 T. finely chopped onion
Few drops Worcestershire sauce
1 t. lemon juice
1 c. dairy sour cream

Combine all ingredients except sour cream. Mix well. Fold in sour cream. Chill. Serve with a green salad.

Mrs. P. I. Parker

QUICKY RUSSIAN DRESSING

½ c. mayonnaise
2 T. catsup

Mix and pour on tossed salad.

PARSLEY OR CHIVE BUTTER

½ c. butter or margarine
1 T. chopped parsley or chives
1 t. paprika
2 t. lemon juice

Cream butter or margarine. Beat in remaining ingredients. If preferred, butter or margarine may be melted, ingredients added and used as a basting or dipping sauce. Yield: about ½ cup.

Note: This butter is good served with sirloin steak.

Mrs. R. T. Webster

DRESSINGS AND SAUCES

TOMATO SOUP SALAD DRESSING

1 can tomato soup
¾ c. sugar
⅓ c. vinegar
1 t. each: celery salt, garlic powder, dry onion, paprika, Worcestershire sauce
½ t. pepper
1 c. salad oil

Mix all ingredients well. Store in refrigerator.

Mrs. T. B. Bolen

POTATO SALAD DRESSING

1 egg, well beaten
½ c. boiling water
1 t. salt
1 heaping t. flour (mixed with a little water)
1 t. dry mustard
½ c. vinegar
½ c. sugar
1 heaping t. butter

Mix all ingredients in top of a double boiler and cook until thick. Add a few drops of yellow food coloring if desired.

Mrs. Chester A. Cramer

COLE SLAW DRESSING

1 c. sugar	2 t. flour
1 c. cider vinegar	2 t. dry mustard
2 eggs, beaten	

Beat together eggs, flour and mustard. Add sugar and vinegar and cook over medium heat until mixture starts to boil. Remove from heat to cool. Place in glass jar and refrigerate. This will keep refrigerated for several months.

Martha Koegel

BARBECUE SAUCE NO. 1

1 10½-oz. can condensed tomato soup
1 c. brown sugar, firmly packed
4 T. butter (½ stick)
4 T. catsup
2 T. prepared mustard
1 t. onion powder
¼ t. garlic powder
2 T. lemon juice
1 T. Worcestershire sauce
2 T. liquid smoke

Combine all ingredients together in a sauce-pan. Simmer over low flame until mixture comes to a boil, stirring frequently. Let boil for 1 minute, remove from heat, use as a zesty sauce for outdoor barbecuing.

Jacqueline Shafer

GREEN TOMATO SOY

2 gals. unpeeled   2 T. salt
  green tomatoes   2 T. pepper
12 large onions   2 T. ground mustard
1 qt. vinegar   1 T. allspice
1 qt. sugar   1 T. cloves

Thinly slice tomatoes and onions. Add remaining ingredients. Mix and stew, stirring often. Put in a stone jar. This sauce is very sweet and very spicy.

Elizabeth P. Nickles

SAUCES

BEEF — Use oil and cooking sherry or Burgundy wine.

LAMB — Onion or garlic and a generous amount of salt.

SPARERIBS — Use oil sparingly with catsup, chili sauce or soy sauce.

CHICKEN AND FISH — Oil and delicate seasoning of herbs.

LEMON-CATSUP SAUCE

¾ c. catsup
1 T. grated lemon peel
1 t. fresh lemon juice
2 T. steak sauce

Combine above ingredients. Pour over corned beef hash patties or hamburgers.

Mrs. L. O. Surrey

BARBECUE SAUCE NO. 2

1 medium-sized onion
2 T. butter
2 T. vinegar
2 T. brown sugar
4 T. lemon juice
1 c. tomato catsup
½ c. chopped fresh parsley
1½ t. prepared mustard
½ c. water
3 T. Worcestershire sauce
  Salt
  Cayenne pepper

Brown onion in butter. Add remaining ingredients. Simmer 30 minutes. Delicious on roast beef, pork or ham barbecues.

Mrs. Lawrence Dedrick

WESTERN SAUCE

¾ c. catsup
⅓ c. chili sauce
2 T. prepared mustard
½ c. brown sugar
½ c. cider vinegar
1 T. salad oil
  Dash hot pepper sauce
2 T. steak sauce
1 clove minced garlic

Combine ingredients and mix well. Yield: about 2¼ cups.

Alice P. Day

TARTAR SAUCE

½ c. mayonnaise or salad dressing
1 T. chopped olives
1 T. chopped onion
1 T. chopped parsley
1 T. chopped sweet pickle

Combine ingredients, mixing well. Chill. Serve over fish.

Katy Baldwin

SPICY FRENCH DRESSING

1 10¾-oz. can tomato soup
¾ c. salad oil
¾ c. sugar
½ c. vinegar
1 small onion, cut up
1 t. Worcestershire sauce
1 small clove garlic (or ½ t. garlic powder)
1 t. salt
¾ t. pepper
¾ t. paprika
½ t. dry mustard

Blend all ingredients together. A blender works best. Dressing keeps in the refrigerator for several weeks. Yield: About 1 quart.

Oliva Petracek

UNCOOKED CHILI SAUCE

1 peck ripe tomatoes (not too ripe)
1 c. salt
2½ lbs. sugar
1 c. grated horseradish
1 qt. vinegar
3 bunches celery
3 onions
3 sweet peppers
2 ozs. mustard seed

Chop tomatoes fine, add salt and let stand overnight. In the morning, drain well. Chop the peppers, onions and celery. Add to the tomato mixture with the sugar, horseradish, vinegar and mustard seeds. Put in jars and seal.

Elizabeth P. Nickles

RELISHES AND PICKLES

MUSTARD AND PEPPER RELISH

5 green peppers   3 large onions
3 red peppers

Grind in food grinder, then drain in strainer for approximately 1 hour.

1 c. flour
6 c. granulated sugar
3 c. vinegar
1 c. water
1 small jar light mustard
2 T. salt
2 t. turmeric
2 t. celery seed

Mix the dry ingredients and spices together. Add mustard and vinegar. Cook until thickened. Cool, then seal with parawax. Yields approximately 6 pints.

Note: This relish can be used on hot dogs, hamburgers, sandwiches, for ham salad or as a dressing for potato salad.

Mrs. Paul J. Clark

CORN AND KRAUT SALAD

1½ c. sugar
 ½ c. white syrup
 1 c. white vinegar
2½ c. sauerkraut
 1 1-lb. can whole kernel corn
 1 small jar red pimientos
 1 green pepper, cut fine
1½ c. celery, chopped fine

Mix first 6 ingredients together. Strain, mash, then drain again. Add pepper and celery. Let stand 24 hours in refrigerator before serving.

Mary C. Hurt

HOMEMADE MUSTARD

2 T. dry mustard   4 T. sugar
4 T. flour

Combine above ingredients. Add enough vinegar to beat smoothly. Sweet pickle juice may be added if desired. Let stand ½ hour or more before using. Add a little more sugar and flour to taste.

Mrs. Kenneth E. Coon

TOMATO CATSUP

 1 peck (12½ pounds) ripe tomatoes
 2 medium onions
 ¼ t. cayenne pepper
 2 c. cider vinegar
1½ T. broken stick cinnamon
 1 T. whole cloves
 3 cloves garlic, finely chopped
 1 T. paprika
 1 c. sugar
2½ t. salt

Wash and slice tomatoes. Boil about 15 minutes or until soft. Into another kettle slice the onions. Cover with a small amount of water and cook until tender. Run the cooked onions and tomatoes through a sieve. Mix the onion and tomato pulp. Add the cayenne pepper. Boil this mixture rapidly until it has been reduced to about half of the original volume.

Place vinegar in an enamel pan: add a spice bag containing the cinnamon, cloves and garlic. Allow this to simmer for about 30 minutes, then bring to boiling point. Place cover on pan and remove from heat. Allow this to stand in covered pan until ready to use.

When tomato mixture has cooked down to half of the original volume, add vinegar mixture, of which there should be 1¼ cups. Add the paprika, sugar and salt and boil rapidly until desired consistency is reached. This should require about 10 minutes rapid boiling. Pour while boiling hot into sterilized jars and seal at once.

Darlene Kronschnabel

BANANA PEPPER RELISH

1 gal. banana peppers
3 c. vinegar
3 c. sugar
1 T. mustard seed
1 small head cabbage, shredded

Chop banana peppers and cabbage. Add mustard seeds and soak overnight in 3 tablespoons salt. Next day, drain; then add sugar and vinegar. Bring to a boil. Put in hot, clean jars.

Note: This colorful relish is delicious with dried beans.

Audrey Little

ARISTOCRAT PICKLES

2 c. pickling salt
4 qts. water
4 qts. thinly sliced cucumbers
  (4 to 5 inches long)
1 T. powdered alum
1 T. ground ginger
2 c. white vinegar
2 c. water
6 c. sugar
1 stick cinnamon
1 t. whole cloves
1 t. celery seed
¼ t. whole allspice

Dissolve salt in the 4 quarts of water. Add cucumbers. Let stand 8 days. On the 9th day, drain well. Add fresh unsalted water to cover. Add alum. Simmer 30 minutes. Drain well. Add fresh water to cover; add ginger. Simmer again 30 minutes. Drain well. Mix vinegar, 2 cups of water, sugar and spices (tie spices in cloth bag). Add cucumbers and simmer again until pickles are clear. Pack in hot, sterilized pint jars. Seal. Makes 6 pints.

Verna Sparks

CANDIED DILLS

I like them with a full course meal,
I like them with my lunch,
I thoroughly enjoy them
With a coffee break or brunch.

They're delightful with a sandwich
And with breakfast they are fine;
And if you really want to know . . .
I'd eat them anytime!

Mrs. Paul E. King

CANDIED DILL PICKLES

1 qt. dill pickles
3 c. extra-fine granulated sugar
⅔ c. tarragon or cider vinegar
2 T. mixed pickling spices

Combine sugar, vinegar and pickling spices in a saucepan. Bring to a boil. Boil 1 minute. Drain, discarding juice in which they were packed. Cut pickles in ¼-inch slices and re-pack in quart jar. Strain out pickling spices and pour warm syrup over pickles. Store in refrigerator 1 week before using. Yield: 1 quart.

Mrs. Paul E. King

DILL PICKLES

Cucumbers, any size or shape, but fresh and firm.

1 c. salt   Dill sprigs
1 qt. cider vinegar   Alum
3 qt. water   Garlic buds (optional)

Make a brine by boiling the salt, vinegar and water 10 minutes. Wash cucumbers in cold water and remove the prickles. Rinse clean jars in hot water, place dill at bottom or on side of jars, one at a time as they are filled. Use proportion of 1 large sprig dill to 1-quart jar. Drop into jars the alum lumps and garlic pieces, to the proportion of 1 lump alum the size of a pea to each pint. Do the same for the garlic. Arrange compactly, small cucumbers in small jars; larger, smooth cucumbers in larger, smooth jars; and odd-shaped cucumber chunks in odd-shaped jars (old but good jam and pickle jars, etc.).

See that the brine is nearly boiling hot. Pour it gently over the cucumbers until jar is full. Place a tight lid on each jar as it is filled. The lids should be sterilized. Old lids can be used if in good condition.

Ruth Bunker Christiansen

BREAD AND BUTTER PICKLES

8 medium onions, sliced thin
2 large sweet peppers, sliced in
  rings or strips
½ c. coarse salt
1 gal. unpeeled cucumbers
5 c. sugar
5 c. vinegar
3 T. mustard seed
1 T. celery seed
½ t. each: ground cloves and turmeric

Cut cucumbers in paper-thin slices. Let onion, peppers, cucumber and salt stand covered with ice water for 3 hours. Drain. Make a syrup from sugar, vinegar and spices. When sugar is dissolved, add drained pickles. Bring to a boil, but do not boil. Pack in sterilized jars.

Juanita Patrick

BARBECUE

Aromas wreathed in hickory smoke
Foretell that scrumptious thrill
Of sizzling, smoky fragrant meat
Cooked on the outdoor grill...
Dad charbroils with special joy
These rich sauce-glazed entrées
Which we have as a festive treat
For warm, bright weekend days.

Andrea Kerry Shafer

INDEX

Notes

ACKNOWLEDGMENT

*Recipes and photographs in Chic
becue and Fish Bake sections
through the courtesy of Reynold
Company.*